THE 2007 CHARLTON COIN GUIDE
46th EDITION

Dealer's buying prices for
Canadian, Newfoundland and Maritime coinage,
Canadian Medals, Tokens and Paper Money,
United States and World Gold Coinage

by
W. K. Cross

Toronto, Ontario • Palm Harbor, Florida

COPYRIGHT AND TRADEMARK NOTICE

© Copyright 1960 - 2007 Charlton International Inc. All rights reserved.

No part of this publication, including Charlton Numbers, may be reproduced, stored in a retrieval system, or transmitted in any form or by any means, digital, electronic, mechanical, photocopying, recording or otherwise, without the prior written permission of the copyright owner.

Permission is hereby given for brief excerpts to be used for the purpose of reviewing this publication in newspapers, magazines, periodicals and bulletins, other than in the advertising of items for sale, provided the source of the material so used is acknowledged in each instance.

While every care has been taken to ensure accuracy in the compilation of the data in this guide, the publisher cannot accept responsibility for typographical errors.

Library and Archives Canada Cataloguing in Publication

Coin guide : a Charlton standard catalogue.

Annual.
46th-
Continues: Charlton coin guide.
ISSN 1719-7244
ISBN 0-88968-319-0 (46th edition)

    1. Coins, Canadian–Catalogs--Periodicals.
    2. Coins–Prices–Canada--Catalogs--Periodicals.

CJ1864.C5114   737.4971   C2006-902321-2

Printed in Canada
in the Province of Ontario

The Charlton Press

Post Office Box 820, Station Willowdale B
North York, Ontario. M2K 2R1 Canada
Tel: 416-488-1418 Fax: 416-488-4656
Tel: 800-442-6042 Fax: 800-442-1542
www.charltonpress.com; E-mail: chpress@charltonpress.com

CONTENTS

Introduction
   Buying and Selling Prices 5
   Handling and Cleaning Coins. 5
   Handling and Cleaning Paper Money . . . 5
   Mint Marks 5
Coins of Canada
   Nova Scotia. 7
   Prince Edward Island. 7
   New Brunswick. 7
   Newfoundland 8
   Province of Canada 12
   Canada 12
      Large Cents 12
      Small Cents 13
      Five Cents Silver 16
      Five Cents Nickel 17
      Ten Cents 20
      Twenty-five Cents 22
      Fifty Cents 28
      Silver Dollars 31
      Nickel Dollars 33
      Nickel Bronze Dollars 34
      Two Dollars 36
      Gold Coins 37
Collectors Issues
   One Cent 38
   Silver Three Cents 38
   Silver Five Cents 38
   Silver Ten Cents. 38
   Silver Twenty-five Cents 39
   Colourized Twenty-five cents 40
   Silver Fifty Cents 42
   Silver Proof-Like Dollars 49
   Cased Nickel Dollars 49
   Cased Silver Dollars. 50
   Silver Loon Dollars 55
   Bronze Dollars 55
   Two Dollars 56
   Five Dollar Coin 57
Five and Ten Dollar Coins
      1976 Montreal Olympic Coins. 60

Eight Dollar Coins 64
Ten Dollar Coins 65
Fifteen Dollar Coins 65
Twenty Dollar Coins 67
Thirty Dollar Coins 76
Gold Coins
   20 Dollar Coins 77
   50 Dollar Coins 77
   75 Dollar Coins 77
   100 Dollar Coins 78
   150 Dollar Coins 81
   175 Dollar Coins 81
   200 Dollar Coins 82
   300 Dollar Coins 83
   350 Dollar Coins 85
Proof Platinum Coins. 86
Collector Sets
   Proof-like Sets 87
   Specimen Sets 89
   Proof Sets 89
Maple Leaf Bullion Coins. 90
Paper Money of Canada
   Province of Canada 91
   Canada 91
   Bank of Canada 96
Canadian Colonial Tokens
   Newfoundland. 106
   Prince Edward Island 107
   Nova Scotia 109
   New Brunswick 112
   Lower Canada 113
   Wellington Tokens. 116
   Upper Canada Tokens. 117
   Province of Canada Tokens 118
   Anonymous and
      Miscellaneous Tokens 119
Canadian Medals 121
Coins of the United States 127
World Gold Coins 142
Appendix 145

INDEX OF DEALERS

Albern Coins and Foreign Exchange Ltd . . . 4
Colonial Acres Coins 150
Gatewest Coin Ltd. 4
Imperial Coin and Stamp Company 151
Marcus & Company Estate Buyers Inc. . . 6, 152
Proof Positive Coins 149
Ted's Collectables 150
Torex 148

Note: Prices in this book are based on gold and silver prices as of August 1st, 2006.

WE BUY COINS
GOLD & SILVER

MAPLE LEAFS • KRUGERRANDS • GOLD BARS • SILVER BARS

We are also buyers of
Historical and Military Medals, Tokens and Paper Money
Deal With Canada's Largest Independant Coin Dealer

GATEWEST COIN LTD.

**OFFICIAL DISTRIBUTORS FOR
THE ROYAL CANADIAN MINT**

MEMBER: CNA (Life), ANA (Life), CAND
Military Collectors Club of Canada, BBB

1711 CORYDON AVENUE
WINNIPEG Manitoba R3N 0J9

TEL: (204) 489-9112   FAX: (204) 489-9118

WE BUY & SELL

MAPLE LEAFS
KRUGERRANDS
GOLD & SILVER BARS

ALBERN COINS
and FOREIGN EXCHANGE LTD.
A GATEWEST GROUP COMPANY

1615 Centre Street North West
CALGARY, Alberta T2E 2S2
FAX 403-276-5415 Information 403-276-8938

INTRODUCTION

It is more difficult to obtain old coins in circulation, much more so than it was twenty-five years ago. For the most part silver no longer circulates, since its bullion value now exceeds its face value. Generally speaking, the only pre-1968 coins in circulation are one-cent and five-cent pieces, and these seldom pre-date 1953. Older coins must now be purchased through dealers.

BUYING AND SELLING PRICES

Buying prices are what dealers pay for coins. Selling prices are what dealers charge for coins. Generally, dealers will pay 40% to 60% of their selling price. It should be remembered all dealers will pay according to their needs. They will pay well for what they need immediately, but for those coins for which there is no demand, even if they have a high retail value, they will offer substantially less.

The prices shown in this book represent averages or estimates of buying prices and should serve as a guide in negotiating fair prices when buying or selling. Also a clearer idea of which coins are in demand by collectors and dealers can be developed by studying the guide.

Coins should not be mailed for appraisal unless a written response to an inquiry is received from the dealer. If coins are mailed, then they should be sent by registered mail, insured, accompanied by a list of the coins sent, with a complete return address and return postage.

HANDLING AND CLEANING COINS

Coins should be handled by the edges only. Avoid touching the surfaces. Many collectors have found too late that fingerprints cannot be removed from coins or other metal valuables. Proof and specimen quality coins must be handled with extra care since their high lustre is very fragile.

Inevitably, the question of whether to clean coins or not will arise. Probably the best course to follow is, when in doubt don't, until you have contacted an experienced collector or dealer.

The tarnish on silver coins can be removed, but it will not necessarily raise the value. If the tarnish is very thick, then its removal could leave the coin looking much worse.

Nickel coins seldom require cleaning, and only soap and water are safe since nickel is a fairly active metal. Copper and bronze should not be cleaned by anyone who is not knowledgeable in the chemical properties of these metals and their alloys.

Whatever the metal, abrasives must never be used. There are many polishes on the market which are designed for silverware, copper and brass. These must not be used with coins. The results are disastrous.

HANDLING AND CLEANING PAPER MONEY

Inexperienced collectors should always use great care when handling notes. Notes should be handled as little as possible, since oil and perspiration from one's skin can damage and devalue a note. Care should be taken to ensure that unfolded or uncreased notes remain so, and that even marginal tears or abrasions are avoided. Under no circumstances should one ever wash or otherwise try to clean a note since it is likely that the note's value will be considerably reduced. The same is true for ironing or pressing. It should be avoided.

MINT MARKS

A mint mark is a letter stamped on a coin to designate the mint that produced the coins.

Canadian decimal coinage issued prior to 1908 was struck at either the Tower Mint, London, in which case it has no mint mark, or at the Heaton Mint in Birmingham. The Birmingham coins have a small "H" as a mint mark. Since 1908 all Canadian coins have been struck at the Ottawa or Winnipeg Mints, with no mint marks, except the Canadian sovereigns which were identified by a small "C" above the date and a "W" when struck at Winnipeg. Newfoundland's coinage was struck at either London, Birmingham, or Ottawa. The Tower Mint coins had no marks, the Birmingham coins had an "H," and the Ottawa coins had a "C," except for the 1940 and 1942 cent pieces.

The coinage of New Brunswick and Nova Scotia had no mint marks because it was struck at the Tower Mint. Prince Edward Island's coinage was struck at Birmingham, but no mint mark was used because the dies were supplied by the Tower Mint.

COMPOSITION MARKS

Beginning in 1999, the Royal Canadian Mint, after years of development began issuing multiply plated steel coinage. Coins made by this new method carry the letter "P", for plated, on the obverse below the Queen's portrait.

SEE US IN YOUR TOWN SOON!

**DOWNSIZING, SETTLING AN ESTATE,
A CHANGE IN LIFESTYLE, MOVING
ALL ARE GOOD REASONS TO CALL
CANADA'S LARGEST BUYER OF ESTATES**

WE CAN OFFER
Immediate hassle-free transactions
Real Buyers with Real Cash Offers
Real Experience with over 25 years of settling estates

US Gold Coins Wanted

5 Carat G, VS1
Paying $65,000

Rolex President
#118238 $12,000

WE WILL BUY
Coins: Silver, Gold, Copper, Canadian, United States & World
Paper Money: Chartered Notes, Dominion & Bank of Canada
Medals: Military Medals, Badges & Awards
Bullion: Gold, Silver, Platinum, From Scrap to .9999
Diamonds: 1 Carat to 6 Carats, Emerald, Ruby & Sapphire
Jewellery: Antique, Estate & Modern Rings, Bracelets, Necklaces, Earrings, Pendants
Sterling Silver: Tea Sets, Trays, Flatware & Holloware
Doulton, Crown Derby, Worcester, Lladro, Beswick & Swarovski
ROLEX, PATEK PHILIPPE, CARTIER, LECOULTRE, IWC
EATON 1/4 CENTURY, OMEGA, BREITLING, VACHERON
GOLD, STEEL & PLATINUM WATCHES
Wrist Watches: Automatic, Manual Wind, Chiming, Musical Perpetual Calendar, Chronograph, Moonphase, Alarm, etc.
Pocket Watches: Repeater, Chiming, Multi-Coloured Railway 21 Jewels or more, Up & Down, Stop & Complicated

**We Need U.S. Silver Dollars & Gold Coins!
We Have Investors Waiting.**

Some of the Cities We Visit Regularly

Brandon	London	Regina	Toronto
Calgary	Moncton	Saint John	Vancouver
Edmonton	Montreal	Saskatoon	Victoria
Halifax	Ottawa	St. John's	Windsor
Hamilton	Quebec City	Thunder Bay	Winnipeg

For More Information on our Cross-country Buying Events:

Marcus & Company Estate Buyers Inc.
#6 - 1131 Gorham Street, Newmarket, Ontario L3Y 8X9
• By Appointment Only •
Tel: (905)895-5005 • Fax: (905)895-2585
email: info@marcusandcompany.com

We Are Canada's Largest Buyers Because We Pay More

COINS OF CANADA

NOVA SCOTIA

VICTORIA 1861 - 1864

Date and Denomination	Buying Price
1861 half cent	4.00
1864 half cent	4.00
1861 one cent	2.50
1862 one cent	30.00
1864 one cent	2.50

PRINCE EDWARD ISLAND

VICTORIA 1871

Date and Denomination	Buying Price
1871 one cent	2.00

NEW BRUNSWICK

VICTORIA 1861 - 1864

Date and Denomination	Buying Price
1861 half cent	85.00
1861 one cent	3.00
1864 one cent	3.00
1862 five cents	40.00
1864 five cents	60.00
1862 ten cents	50.00
1864 ten cents	60.00
1862 twenty cents	20.00
1864 twenty cents	25.00

IMPORTANT: Buying prices are listed for coins graded VG or better. Bent, damaged or badly worn coins are not collectable and bring no premium value.

NEWFOUNDLAND

LARGE CENTS

Wide 0   Narrow 0

GEORGE V 1913 - 1936

Date and Mint Mark	Buying Price
1913	.75
1917C	.75
1919C	.75
1920C	.75
1929	.75
1936	.75

VICTORIA 1865 - 1896

Date and Mint Mark	Description	Buying Price
1865		3.00
1872H		2.50
1873		3.00
1876H		3.00
1880	Wide 0	2.50
1880	Narrow 0	110.00
1885		22.00
1888		22.00
1890		2.50
1894		2.50
1896		2.50

SMALL CENTS

GEORGE VI 1938 - 1947

Date and Mint Mark	Description	Buying Price
1938		.15
1940		.30
1940	Re-engraved Date	15.00
1941C		.15
1942		.15
1943C		.15
1944C		.30
1947C		.15

EDWARD VII 1904 - 1909

Date and Mint Mark	Buying Price
1904H	5.00
1907	1.50
1909	1.50

FIVE CENTS

VICTORIA 1865 - 1880

Date and Mint Mark	Buying Price
1865	30.00
1870	50.00
1872H	25.00
1873	100.00
1873H	825.00
1876H	75.00
1880	35.00

VICTORIA 1881 - 1896

Date and Mint Mark	Buying Price
1881	30.00
1882H	20.00
1885	125.00
1888	30.00
1890	7.00
1894	7.00
1896	4.00

EDWARD VII 1903 - 1908

Date and Mint Mark	Buying Price
1903	3.00
1904H	2.00
1908	3.00

GEORGE V 1912 - 1929

Date and Mint Mark	Buying Price
1912	.75
1917C	.75
1919C	3.00
1929	.75

GEORGE VI 1938 - 1947

Date and Mint Mark	Buying Price
1938	.60
1940C	.60
1941C	.60
1942C	.60
1943C	.60
1944C	.60
1945C	.60
1946C	225.00
1947C	.60

TEN CENTS

VICTORIA 1865 - 1896

Date and Mint Mark	Buying Price
1865	20.00
1870	100.00
1872H	15.00
1873	35.00
1876H	25.00
1880	30.00
1882H	25.00
1885	75.00
1888	25.00
1890	7.00
1894	7.00
1896	7.00

EDWARD VII 1903 - 1904

Date and Mint Mark	Buying Price
1903	4.00
1904H	2.00

GEORGE V 1912 -1919

Date and Mint Mark	Buying Price
1912	.75
1917C	.75
1919C	1.00

IMPORTANT: Buying prices are listed for coins graded VG or better. Bent, damaged or badly worn coins are not collectable and bring no premium value.

GEORGE VI 1938 - 1947

Date and Mint Mark	Buying Price
1938	.50
1940	.50
1941C	.50
1942C	.50
1943C	.50
1944C	.50
1945C	.50
1946C	1.00
1947C	.50

TWENTY CENTS

VICTORIA 1865 - 1900

Date and Mint Mark	Buying Price
1865	12.00
1870	15.00
1872H	10.00
1873	20.00
1876H	20.00
1880	20.00
1881	15.00
1882H	15.00
1885	15.00
1888	7.00
1890	7.00
1894	7.00
1896	7.00
1899	5.00
1900	5.00

EDWARD VII 1904

Date and Mint Mark	Buying Price
1904H	9.00

GEORGE V 1912

Date and Mint Mark	Buying Price
1912	1.00

TWENTY-FIVE CENTS

GEORGE V 1917 - 1919

Date and Mint Mark	Buying Price
1917C	1.10
1919C	1.10

IMPORTANT: A mint mark is a letter stamped on a coin to designate the mint that produced the coin. The Canadian Mint used the letter "C" or "W," while the Heaton Mint in England used the letter "H."

IMPORTANT: Buying prices listed are for coins graded VG or better. Bent, damaged or badly worn coins are not collectable and bring no premium over the silver value.

FIFTY CENTS

VICTORIA 1870 - 1900

Date and Mint Mark	Buying Price
1870	15.00
1872H	12.00
1873	35.00
1874	35.00
1876H	25.00
1880	25.00
1881	17.00
1882H	10.00
1885	25.00
1888	35.00
1894	10.00
1896	7.00
1898	7.00
1899	7.00
1900	7.00

EDWARD VII 1904 - 1909

Date and Mint Mark	Buying Price
1904H	3.00
1907	3.00
1908	3.00
1909	3.00

GEORGE V 1911 - 1919

Date and Mint Mark	Buying Price
1911	3.00
1917C	3.00
1918C	3.00
1919C	3.00

TWO DOLLARS GOLD

VICTORIA 1865 - 1888

Date and Mint Mark	Buying Price
1865	175.00
1870	175.00
1872	200.00
1880	800.00
1881	150.00
1882H	150.00
1885	150.00
1888	150.00

Note: Two dollar gold coins must be VF condition or better. Damaged, bent or holed coins are bought for gold content.

PROVINCE OF CANADA

LARGE CENTS

Wide 9 over 8   Narrow 9

VICTORIA 1858 - 1859

Date and Mint Mark	Description	Buying Price
1858		35.00
1859	Narrow 9	2.00
1859	* Brass N9	1,500.00
1859	W/9 over 8	20.00

FIVE CENTS

Large date   Small date

VICTORIA 1858

Date and Mint Mark	Description	Buying Price
1858	Small Date	12.00
1858	Large Date	100.00

TEN CENTS

VICTORIA 1858

Date and Mint Mark	Buying Price
1858	15.00
1858 8/5	400.00

Note: * Brass metal is yellow in colour.

TWENTY CENTS

VICTORIA 1858

Date and Mint Mark	Buying Price
1858	50.00

CANADA

LARGE CENTS

 Small date Small leaves   Large date Large leaves

VICTORIA 1876 - 1901

Date and Mint Mark	Description	Buying Price
1876H		2.00
1881H		3.00
1882H		3.00
1884		2.00
1886		2.50
1887		2.00
1888		2.00
1890H		4.00
1891	Large Leaves, Large Date	4.00
1891	Large Leaves, Small Date	40.00
1891	Small Leaves, Small Date	60.00
1892		3.00
1893		2.00
1894		5.00
1895		2.00
1896		1.50
1897		1.50
1898H		3.00
1899		2.00
1900		4.00
1900H		1.50
1901		1.50

1936 Dot

EDWARD VII 1902 - 1910

Date and Mint Mark	Buying Price
1902	.75
1903	.75
1904	.75
1905	.75
1906	.75
1907	.75
1907H	4.00
1908	.75
1909	.75
1910	.75

GEORGE V 1920 - 1936

Date and Mint Mark	Description	Buying Price
1920		.05
1921		.05
1922		7.00
1923		16.00
1924		3.00
1925		13.00
1926		2.50
1927		.05
1928		.05
1929		.05
1930		.50
1931		.10
1932		.05
1933		.05
1934		.05
1935		.05
1936		.05
1936	Dot	50,000.00

Note: The 1936 Dot one cent coin is very rare, only four are confirmed. Examples must be authenticated and certified as counterfiet examples do exist.

GEORGE V 1911 - 1920

Date and Mint Mark	Buying Price
1911	.20
1912	.20
1913	.20
1914	.20
1915	.20
1916	.20
1917	.20
1918	.20
1919	.20
1920	.20

SMALL CENTS

1947 Maple Leaf Blunt 7   1947 Maple Leaf Pointed 7

GEORGE VI 1937 - 1947

Date and Mint Mark	Description	Buying Price
1937 to 1947		.01
1947	Maple Leaf, Blunt 7	.10
1947	Maple Leaf, Pointed 7	.01

"A" points to denticles   "A" points between denticles

GEORGE VI 1948 - 1952

Date and Mint Mark	Description	Buying Price
1948	"A" Points to	.01
1948	"A" Between	.10
1949	"A" Points to	15.00
1949	"A" Between	.01
1950 to 1952		.01

Centennial

ELIZABETH II, TIARA PORTRAIT, 1965 - 1981

Date and Mint Mark	Description	Buying Price
1965 to 1966		.01
1967	Centennial	.01
1968 to 1981		.01

Blunt 5   Pointed 5

No shoulder fold   Shoulder Fold

ELIZABETH II, TIARA PORTRAIT, 1982 - 1989

Date and Mint Mark	Description	Buying Price
1982 to 1984		.01
1985	Blunt 5	.01
1985	Pointed 5	1.00
1986 to 1989		.01

ELIZABETH II, LAUREATED PORTRAIT, 1953 - 1964

Date and Mint Mark	Description	Buying Price
1953	NSF	.01
1953	SF	.50
1954	SF	.01
1955	NSF	50.00
1955	SF	.01
1956 to 1964		.01

1867 - 1992

ELIZABETH II, DIADEMED PORTRAIT, 1990 - 1996

Date and Mint Mark	Description	Buying Price
1990 to 1991		.01
1867-1992	Double Date	.01
1993 to 1996		.01

Note: You must sort and identify your own coins. Do not expect a dealer to spend hours sorting them for you.

Copper Coinage

Plated Coinage

ELIZABETH II, DIADEMED PORTRAIT, 1997 - 2003

Date and Mint Mark	Description	Buying Price
1997 to 2001		.01
1952-2002	Double Date	.01
2003		.01

Composition Mark

ELIZABETH II, DIADEMED PORTRAIT, 1999P - 2003P

Date and Mint Mark	Description	Buying Price
1999P	Not Issued	5.00
2000P	Not Issued	1,000.00
2001P	Not Issued	.01
1952-2002P	Double Date	.01
2003P		.01

ELIZABETH II, MATURE PORTRAIT, 2003 - 2006

Date and Mint Mark	Buying Price
2003	.01
2004	.01
2005	.01
2006	.01

ELIZABETH II, MATURE PORTRAIT, 2003P - 2006P

Date and Mint Mark	Buying Price
2003P	.01
2004P	.01
2005P	.01
2006P	.01

Note: The 2000P one cent was issued to vending companies for test purposes.

FIVE CENTS SILVER

1874 Plain 4   **1874** Crosslet 4

1875 1875H Small date Short top on 5   **1875** 1875H Large date Long top on 5

1900 1900 Small Date   **1900** 1900 Large Date

Small H   Large H

Small 8   Large 8

Maple   Holly

EDWARD VII 1902 - 1910

Date and Mint Mark	Description	Buying Price
1902	Plain	1.00
1902	Large H	1.00
1902	Small H	5.00
1903H	Large H	12.00
1903H	Small H	1.00
1903		2.00
1904		1.00
1905		1.00
1906		1.00
1907		1.00
1908	Small 8	3.00
1908	Large 8	15.00
1909	Maple Leaves	1.00
1909	Holly Leaves	10.00
1910	Maple Leaves	5.00
1910	Holly Leaves	1.00

VICTORIA 1870 - 1901

Date and Mint Mark	Description	Buying Price
1870		10.00
1871		10.00
1872H		8.00
1874H	Plain 4	15.00
1874H	Crosslet 4	15.00
1875H	Small Date	100.00
1875H	Large Date	150.00
1880H		5.00
1881H		5.00
1882H		7.00
1883H		15.00
1884		100.00
1885		8.00
1886		7.00
1887		12.00
1888		4.00
1889		15.00
1890H		3.00
1891		3.00
1892		3.00
1893		3.00
1894		15.00
1896		3.00
1897		4.00
1898		8.00
1899		4.00
1900	Large Date	15.00
1900	Small Date	3.00
1901		3.00

Note: Buying prices are for coins in **Very Good (VG)** condition.

GEORGE V 1911 - 1921

Date and Mint Mark	Buying Price
1911	.75
1912	.75
1913	.75
1914	.75
1915	6.00
1916	.75
1917	.75
1918	.75
1919	.75
1920	.75
1921	1,500.00

FIVE CENTS NICKEL

Near 6   Far 6

GEORGE V 1922 - 1936

Date and Mint Mark	Description	Buying Price
1922 to 1924		.07
1925		45.00
1926	Near 6	1.00
1926	Far 6	75.00
1927 to 1936		.07

Tombac Beaver   Tombac "V"

1947 Maple Leaf   1947 Dot

GEORGE VI 1937 - 1947

Date and Mint Mark	Description	Buying Price
1937	Dot	.05
1938 to 1941		.05
1942	Nickel	.05
1942	Tombac Beaver	.15
1943	Tombac V	.07
1944	Tombav V *	10,000.00
1944 to 1945	Steel V	.10
1946 to 1947		.05
1947	Maple Leaf	.05
1947	Dot	10.00

Geo. VI Obverse   Beaver

1951 High Relief   1951 Comm.

A in GRATIA points to a rim denticle   A in GRATIA points between rim denticles

GEORGE VI 1948 - 1952

Date and Mint Mark	Description	Buying Price
1948	Without "ET IND:IMP"	.05
1949 to 1950		.05
1951	Commemorative	.05
1951	High Relief	200.00
1952		.05

 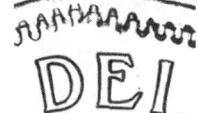

No Shoulder Fold
On the obverse note the flared ends of "I" and the closed top of the "E"

Shoulder Fold
On the obverse note the straight-sided "I" and the open top the the "E"

Note: * This 1944 five cent coin is made of the alloy Tombac. It is brassy in colour when new, and brown when used. It is not the common steel composition of 1944.

Far Maple Leaf Near Maple Leaf

ELIZABETH II, LAUREATED PORTRAIT, 1953 - 1962

Date and Mint Mark	Description	Buying Price
1953	NSF, far	.05
1953	NSF, near	200.00
1953	SF, near	.05
1953	SF, far	100.00
1954	NSF	3,000.00
1954SF to 1962		.05

1964 Extra Water Line

ELIZABETH II, LAUREATED PORTRAIT, 1963 - 1964

Date and Mint Mark	Description	Buying Price
1963 to 1964		.05
1964	Extra Water Line	5.00

1965 Small Beads Attached Jewel   1965 Large Beads Detached Jewel

ELIZABETH II, TIARA PORTRAIT, 1965 - 1966

Date and Mint Mark	Description	Buying Price
1965	Small Beads	.05
1965	Large Beads	25.00
1966		.05

ELIZABETH II, TIARA PORTRAIT, 1967 - 1989

Date and Mint Mark	Description	Buying Price
1967	Centennial	.05
1968 to 1989		.05

1867-1992

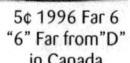

5¢ 1996 Far 6 "6" Far from "D" in Canada

5¢ 1996 Near 6 "6" Near "D" in Canada

Note: You must sort and identify your own coins. Do not expect a dealer to spend hours sorting then for you.

ELIZABETH II, DIADEMED PORTRAIT, 1990 - 2001

Date and Mint Mark	Description	Buying Price
1990		.05
1991		.05
1867-1992	Double Date	.05
1993		.05
1994		.05
1995		.05
1996	Far 6	.05
1996	Near 6	.05
1997		.05
1998		.05
1999		.05
2000		.05
2001		.05

Victory
1945-2005

Plated Coinage

ELIZABETH II, MATURE PORTRAIT, 2003P - 2006P

Date and Mint Mark	Description	Buying Price
2003P	Beaver	.05
2004P	Beaver	.05
2005P	Beaver	.05
2005P	Victory, 1945-2005	.05
2006P	Beaver	.05

 Composition Mark

Double dates 1952 2002P

ELIZABETH II, DIADEMED PORTRAIT, 2000P - 2003P

Date and Mint Mark	Description	Buying Price
2000P		.10
2001P		.05
1952-2002P	Double Date	.05
2003P		.05

TEN CENTS

1870 Narrow "0"
Sides of equal thickness

1870 Wide "0"
Right side is thicker

1886 Small 6

1886 Large,
Pointed 6

1886 Large,
Knobbed 6

1892
2 over 1
Large 9

1892
Normal Date
Small 9

1893
Flat-top 3
Medium 9

1893
Round-top 3
Large 9

1899
Small 9s

1899
Large 9s

VICTORIA 1870 -1901

Date and Mint Mark	Description	Buying Price
1870	Narrow 0	12.00
1870	Wide 0	15.00
1871		20.00
1871H		20.00
1872H		60.00
1874H		12.00
1875H		160.00

VICTORIA 1870 - 1901 (cont.)

Date and Mint Mark	Description	Buying Price
1880H		12.00
1881H		15.00
1882H		15.00
1883H		40.00
1884		160.00
1885		35.00
1886	Small 6	20.00
1886	Large pointed 6	60.00
1886	Large knobbed 6	25.00
1887		30.00
1888		10.00
1889		350.00
1890H		15.00
1891		15.00
1892	Large 9	100.00
1892	Small 9	20.00
1893	Flat Top 3	25.00
1893	Round Top 3	500.00
1894		20.00
1896		8.00
1898		8.00
1899	Small 9	6.00
1899	Large 9	15.00
1900		6.00
1901		6.00

EDWARD VII 1902 - 1910

Date and Mint Mark	Description	Buying Price
1902		5.00
1902H		3.00
1903		10.00
1903H		5.00
1904		6.00
1905		5.00
1906		4.00
1907		3.00
1908		6.00
1909	Victorian Leaves	4.00
1909	Broad Leaves	5.00
1910		3.00

Note: Buying prices are for coins in **Very Good (VG)** condition. Coins of lower grades will command lower prices.

Small Leaves   Broad leaves

GEORGE V 1911 - 1936

Date and Mint Mark	Description	Buying Price
1911		3.00
1912		.45
1913	Small Leaves	.45
1913	Broad Leaves	60.00
1914 to 1936		.45

GEORGE VI 1937 - 1947

Date and Mint Mark	Description	Buying Price
1937 to 1947		.40
1947	Maple Leaf	.40

GEORGE VI 1948 - 1952

Date and Mint Mark	Description	Buying Price
1948	Without "ET IND"IMP"	.40
1949 to 1952		.40

ELIZABETH II, LAUREATED PORTRAIT, 1953 - 1964

Date and Mint Mark		Buying Price
1953 to 1964		.40

1969 Small Date   1969 Large Date

1980 Wide 0   1980 Narrow 0

ELIZABETH II, TIARA PORTRAIT, 1965 - 1989

Date and Mint Mark	Description	Buying Price
1965 to 1966		.40
1967	Centennial	.35
1968	.500 Fine Silver	.25
1968	Nickel	.10
1969	Large Date	7,000.00
1969	Small Date	.10
1970 to 1979		.10
1980	Wide 0	1.00
1980	Narrow 0	.10
1981 to 1989		.10

1867-1992

ELIZABETH II, DIADEMED PORTRAIT, 1990 - 2000

Date and Mint Mark	Description	Buying Price
1990 to 1991		.10
1992	Double Date	.10
1993 to 2000		.10

Plated Coinage

Composition Mark

Year of the Volunteer

Double dates 1952 2002P

ELIZABETH II, DIADEMED PORTRAIT
1999P - 2003P

Date and Mint Mark	Description	Buying Price
1999P		5.00
2000P		300.00
2001P	Volunteers	.10
2001P	Bluenose	.10
1952-2002P	Double Date	.10
2003P		.10

ELIZABETH II, MATURE PORTRAIT, 2003P - 2006P

Date and Mint Mark	Buying Price
2003P	.10
2004P	.10
2005P	.10
2006P	.10

TWENTY-FIVE CENTS

Narrow 0   Wide 0

6 over 3   6 over 6

VICTORIA 1870 - 1901

Date and Mint Mark	Description	Buying Price
1870		12.00
1871		17.00
1871H		16.00
1872H		8.00
1874H		7.00
1875H		225.00
1880H	Narrow O	50.00
1880H	Wide O	125.00
1881H		15.00
1882H		17.00
1883H		12.00
1885		85.00
1886		30.00
1886	6 over 3	35.00
1886	6 over 6	35.00
1887		85.00
1888		15.00
1889		85.00
1890H		20.00
1891		75.00
1892		10.00
1893		85.00
1894		20.00
1899		8.00
1900		8.00
1901		6.00

1947 Dot   1947 Maple Leaf

Small crown   Large crown

GEORGE VI 1937 - 1947

Date and Mint Mark	Description	Buying Price
1937 to 1947		1.00
1947	Maple Leaf	1.00
1947	Dot	20.00

EDWARD VII 1902 - 1910

Date and Mint Mark	Description	Buying Price
1902		5.00
1902H		4.00
1903		5.00
1904		10.00
1905		7.00
1906	Small Crown	500.00
1906	Large Crown	5.00
1907		4.00
1908		8.00
1909		4.00
1910		3.00

GEORGE VI 1948 - 1952

Date and Mint Mark	Descripton	Buying Price
1948	Without "ET IND:IMP"	1.00
1949 to 1952		1.00

GEORGE V 1911 - 1936

Date and Mint Mark	Description	Buying Price
1911		4.00
1912 to 1914		1.25
1915		10.00
1916 to 1920		1.25
1921		6.00
1927		15.00
1928 to 1936		1.25
1936	Dot	15.00

ELIZABETH II, LAUREATED PORTRAIT, 1953 - 1964

Date and Mint Mark	Description	Buying Price
1953	Large Date	1.00
1953	Small Date	1.00
1954 to 1964		1.00

Note: Buying prices are for coins in **Very Good (VG)** condition. Coins with excessive wear, holed or bent will be discount from the listed price.

Note: Victoria, Edward and George V quarters must be Very **Good (VG)** or better.

Centennial   RCMP

1973 Small Bust   1973 Large Bust
120 Obverse Beads   132 Obverse Beads
Far from Rim   Near Rim

ELIZABETH II, TIARA PORTRAIT, 1965 - 1973

Date and Mint Mark	Description	Buying Price
1965 to 1966		1.00
1967	Centennial	.85
1968	.500 Fine Silver	.65
1968 to 1972	Nickel	.25
1973	Small Bust	.25
1973	Large Bust	65.00

ELIZABETH II, TIARA PORTRAIT, 1974 - 1989

Date and Mint Mark	Buying Price
1974 to 1989	.25

ELIZABETH II, DIADEMED PORTRAIT, 1990 - 1991

Date and Mint Mark	Buying Price
1990	.25
1991	1.00

CANADA 125 ANNIVERSARY

Common Obverse

New Brunswick   Northwest Territories

Newfoundland   Manitoba

Yukon   Alberta

Prince Edward Island

Ontario

Nova Scotia

Quebec

Saskatchewan

British Columbia

ELIZABETH II, DIADEMED PORTRAIT, 1992

Date and Mint Mark	Description	Buying Price
1992	New Brunswick, Medal	.25
1992	New Brunswick, Coinage	15.00
1992	Northwest Territories	.25
1992	Newfoundland	.25
1992	Manitoba	.25
1992	Yukon	.25
1992	Alberta	.25
1992	Prince Edward Island	.25
1992	Ontario	.25
1992	Nova Scotia	.25
1992	Quebec	.25
1992	Saskatchewan	.25
1992	British Columbia	.25

ELIZABETH II, DIADEMED PORTRAIT, 1993 - 2001

Date and Mint Mark	Description	Buying Price
1993 to 1996		.25
2001		.25

1999 MILLENNIUM QUARTERS

Common Obverse

January   February

March   April

May   June

July   August

September   October

| | November | | December | | May | | June |

ELIZABETH II, DIADEMED PORTRAIT, 1999

Date and Mint Mark	Description	Buying Price
1999	January	.25
1999	February	.25
1999	March	.25
1999	April	.25
1999	May	.25
1999	June	.25
1999	July	.25
1999	August	.25
1999	September	.25
1999	October	.25
1999	November	.25
1999	December	.25

July   August

September   October

2000 MILLENNIUM QUARTERS

Common Obverse

November   December

ELIZABETH II, DIADEMED PORTRAIT, 2000

Date and Mint Mark	Description	Buying Price
2000	January, Pride	.25
2000	February, Ingenuity	.25
2000	March, Achievement	.25
2000	April, Health	.25
2000	May, Natural Legacy	.25
2000	June, Harmony	.25
2000	July, Celebration	.25
2000	August, Family	.25
2000	September, Wisdom	.25
2000	October. Creativity	.25
2000	November, Freedom	.25
2000	December, Community	.25

January   February

March   April

Note: If a date is not listed then it was not issed for circulation.

Plated Coinage

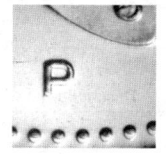
Composition Mark

ELIZABETH II, DIADEMED PORTRAIT, 1999P - 2001P

Date and Mint Mark	Buying Price
1999P	5.00
2000P	1,200.00
2001P	.25

ELIZABETH II, DIADEMED PORTRAIT, 2002P - 2003P

Date and Mint Mark	Description	Buying Price
1952-2002P	Canada Day, Double Date	.25
1952-2002P	Caribou, Double Date	.25
2003P		.25

ELIZABETH II, MATURE PORTRAIT, 2003P - 2006P

Date and Mint Mark	Buying Price
2003P	.25
2004P	.25
2005P	.25
2006P	.25

First Settlement 2004   Poppy 2004

Alberta 2005   Saskatchewan 2005

Year of the Veteran 2006   Breast Cancer 2006

ELIZABETH II, MATURE PORTRAIT, 2004P - 2006P

Date and Mint Mark	Description	Buying Price
2004P	First Settlement	.25
2004P	Poppy	.25
2005P	Caribou	.25
2005P	Alberta	.25
2005P	Saskatchewan	.25
2005P	Year of the Veteran	.25
2006P	Caribou	.25
2006P	Breast Cancer	.25

FIFTY CENTS

L.C.W.   No L.C.W.

VICTORIA 1870 - 1901

Date and Mint Mark	Description	Buying Price
1870	Without L.C.W.	400.00
1870	With L.C.W.	30.00
1871		50.00
1871H		75.00
1872H		30.00
1881H		40.00
1888		150.00
1890H		600.00
1892		50.00
1894		200.00
1898		40.00
1899		100.00
1900		30.00
1901		40.00

EDWARD VII 1902 - 1910

Date and Mint Mark	Description	Buying Price
1902		12.00
1903H		12.00
1904		85.00
1905		85.00
1906		12.00
1907		9.00
1908		15.00
1909		12.00
1910	Victorian Leaves	9.00
1910	Edwardian Leaves	9.00

GEORGE V 1911 - 1936

Date and Mint Mark	Description	Buying Price
1911		12.00
1912		10.00
1913		10.00
1914		10.00
1916		3.00
1917		3.00
1918		3.00
1919		3.00
1920	Wide 0	5.00
1920	Narrow 0	4.00
1921		15,000.00
1929		5.00
1931		10.00
1932		85.00
1934		8.00
1936		15.00

Straight "7"   Curved "7"
No Maple Leaf   No Maple Leaf

Straight "7"   Curved "7"
With Maple Leaf   With Maple Leaf

Note: Coins must grade **Very Good** or better. Badly worn coins (good) will be priced lower.

GEORGE VI 1937 - 1947

Date and Mint Mark	Description	Buying Price
1937 to 1946		2.10
1947	Straight "7"	2.10
1947	Curved "7"	2.10
1947	M.L., Straight "7"	12.00
1947	M.L., Curved "7"	600.00

ELIZABETH II, LAUREATED PORTRAIT, 1953 - 1964

Date and Mint Mark	Description	Buying Price
1953	NSF, SD	2.10
1953	NSF, LD	3.00
1953	SF, LD	2.10
1954 to 1964		2.10

GEORGE VI 1948 - 1952

Date and Mint Mark	Description	Buying Price
1948	Without "ET IND:IMP"	30.00
1949 to 1952		2.10

ELIZABETH II, TIARA PORTRAIT, 1965 - 1967

Date and Mint Mark	Description	Buying Price
1965 to 1966		2.10
1967	Centennial	2.10

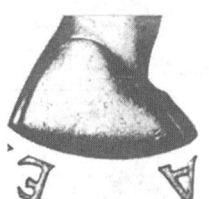
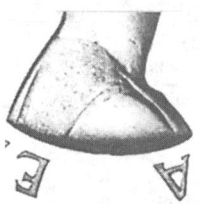

No shoulder fold   Shoulder fold

Small date   Large date

1978 Square Jewels

1978 Round Jewels

1982 - 118 Large Beads

1982 - 120 Small beads

ELIZABETH II, TIARA PORTRAIT, 1968 - 1989

Date and Mint Mark	Description	Buying Price
1968 to 1977		.50
1978	Square Jewels	.50
1978	Round Jewels	1.00
1979 to 1981		.50
1982	Large Beads	.50
1982	Small Beads	10.00
1983 to 1989		.50

ELIZABETH II, DIADEMED PORTRAIT, 1990 - 2000

Date and Mint Mark	Description	Buying Price
1990 to 1991		.50
1867-1992	Double Date	.50
1993 to 1996		.50
1997 to 2000	Modified Reverse	.50

Plated Coinage

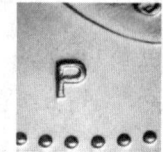
Composition Mark

ELIZABETH II, DIADEMED PORTRAIT, 1999P - 2001P

Date and Mint Mark	Buying Price
1999P	5.00
2000P	2,000.00
2001P	.50

ELIZABETH II, IMPERIAL STATE CROWN PORTRAIT, 2002P

Date and Mint Mark	Description	Buying Price
1952-2002P	Jubilee Portrait	.50

ELIZABETH II, MATURE PORTRAIT, 2005P - 2006P

Date and Mint Mark	Buying Price
2005P	.50
2006P	.50

SILVER DOLLARS

1935 Obverse

1936 Obverse

1937 to 1947 Obverse

1935 Reverse

1939 Parliament

1949 Newfoundland

Blunt 7   Pointed 7

1947 Maple Leaf

1947 Dot

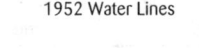

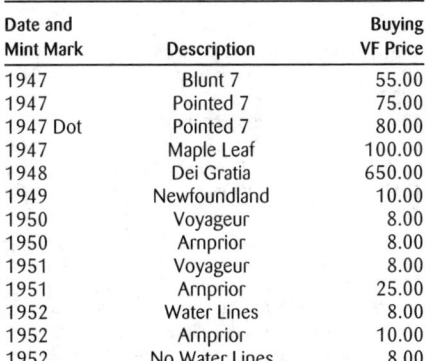
1952 Water Lines   1952 No Water Lines

GEORGE V 1935 - 1936

Date and Mint Mark	Description	Buying VF Price
1935	Silver Jubilee	15.00
1936	Voyageur	10.00

GEORGE VI 1937 - 1946

Date and Mint Mark	Description	Buying VF Price
1937	Voyageur	10.00
1938	Voyageur	30.00
1939	Royal Visit	8.00
1945	Voyageur	90.00
1946	Voyageur	20.00

GEORGE VI 1947 - 1952

Date and Mint Mark	Description	Buying VF Price
1947	Blunt 7	55.00
1947	Pointed 7	75.00
1947 Dot	Pointed 7	80.00
1947	Maple Leaf	100.00
1948	Dei Gratia	650.00
1949	Newfoundland	10.00
1950	Voyageur	8.00
1950	Arnprior	8.00
1951	Voyageur	8.00
1951	Arnprior	25.00
1952	Water Lines	8.00
1952	Arnprior	10.00
1952	No Water Lines	8.00

IMPORTANT: The silver dollar buying prices are for problem free coins in **Very Fine (VF)** condition. Damaged coins will bring lower prices.

1953 Obverse    1959 Reverse    1964 Charlottetown

1958 British Columbia    1965 Reverse    1967 Centennial

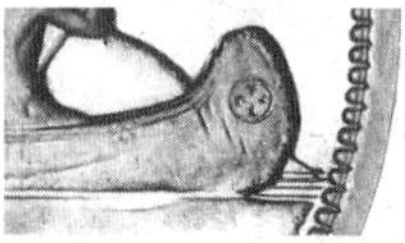

1955 4 Water Lines    1955 2 ½ Water Lines 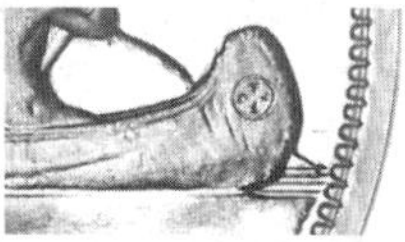   1957 4 Water Lines 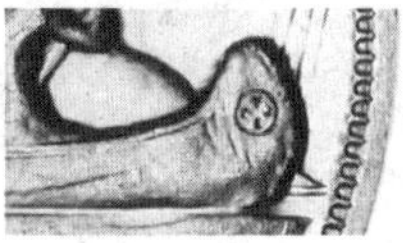   1957 2 ½ Water Lines

ELIZABETH II, LAUREATED PORTRAIT, 1953 - 1964			ELIZABETH II, TIARA PORTRAIT, 1965 - 1967		
Date and Mint Mark	Description	Buying VF Price	Date and Mint Mark	Description	Buying VF Price
1953	Voyageur	8.00	1961	Voyageur	8.00
1954	Voyageur	8.00	1962	Voyageur	8.00
1955	Voyageur	8.00	1963	Voyageur	8.00
1955 Arnprior	2 ½ Waterlines	35.00	1964	Charlottetown	8.00
1956	Voyageur	8.00	1965	Voyageur, Medal	8.00
1957	Voyageur	8.00	1965	Voyageur, Coinage	1,000.00
1957 Arnprior	One Waterline	8.00	1966	Voyageur	8.00
1958	British Columbia	8.00	1966 Sm Beads	Voyageur	1,750.00
1959	Voyageur	8.00	1967	Centennial, Medal	8.00
1960	Voyageur	8.00	1967	Centennial, Coinage	1,000.00

DIE AXIS

The obverse design is considered the primary side of the coin. The die axis is the relationship of the reverse design to the obverse. Consider the obverse die, usually the anvil die in a press, stationary and when installed is the point of reference. The reverse die (moving hammer die) may be turned or set at any of 360 degrees in relation to the set obverse die. If the obverse die is identified by an upright arrow (↑) then the reverse die may be represented by a second arrow(↑). These arrows form a relationship. Illustrated below are two common die positions:

Coinage Axis: ↑↓
   Obverse die: ↑
   Reverse die is set 180 degrees opposite: ↓

Medal Axis: ↑↑
   Obverse die:
   Reverse die is set in the matching direction: ↑

NICKEL DOLLARS

Common Obverse

Voyageur Reverse

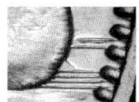
1968 Island

1968 No Island

Manitoba

British Columbia

Prince Edward Island

Winnipeg

Constitution

Jacques Cartier

ELIZABETH II, TIARA PORTRAIT, 1968 - 1973		
Date and Mint Mark	Description	Buying Price
1968	Voyageur	1.00
1968	Small Island	1.25
1968	No Island	2.00
1969	Voyageur	1.00
1970	Manitoba	1.00
1971	British Columbia	1.00
1972	Voyageur	1.00
1973	P.E.I.	1.00

ELIZABETH II, TIARA PORTRAIT, 1974 - 1986		
Date and Mint Mark	Description	Buying Price
1974	Winnipeg	1.00
1975 to 1981	Voyageur	1.00
1982	Constitution, Medal	1.00
1982	Consitution, Coinage	250.00
1983	Voyageur	1.00
1984	Jacques Cartier	1.00
1985	Voyageur	1.00
1986	Voyageur	1.00

NICKEL BRONZE DOLLARS

ELIZABETH II, TIARA PORTRAIT, 1987 - 1989

Date and Mint Mark	Description	Buying Price
1987	Loon, Unc	1.00
1987	Loon, Proof	4.00
1988	Loon	1.00
1989	Loon	1.00

ELIZABETH II, DIADEMED PORTRAIT, 1992 - 1993

Date and Mint Mark	Description	Buying Price
1867-1992	Double Date	1.00
1993	Loon	1.00

ELIZABETH II, DIADEMED PORTRAIT, 1990 - 1991

Date and Mint Mark	Description	Buying Price
1990 to 1991	Loon	1.00

ELIZABETH II, DIADEMED PORTRAIT, 1994

Date and Mint Mark	Description	Buying Price
1994	Remembrance, Unc	1.00
1994	Remembrance, Proof	4.00
1994	Loon	1.00

CANADA 125 ANNIVERSARY

ELIZABETH II, DIADEMED PORTRAIT, 1992

Date and Mint Mark	Description	Buying Price
1992	Unc	1.00

ELIZABETH II, DIADEMED PORTRAIT, 1995

Date and Mint Mark	Description	Buying Price
1995	Peacekeeping, Unc	1.00
1995	Peacekeeping, Proof	4.00

IMPORTANT: Do not clean your coins. Coins should be handled carefully. Only experts should consider cleaning. If you are not an expert, the results can be disastrous.

Note: Proof issues of 1987, 1992, 1994 and 1995 were issued by the Numismatic Deptartment of the Royal Canadian Mint.

ELIZABETH II, DIADEMED PORTRAIT, 1995 - 1996

Date and Mint Mark	Description	Buying Price
1995	Loon	1.00
1996	Loon	1.00

2004 Lucky Loonie   2005 Terry Fox

ELIZABETH II, DIADEMED PORTRAIT, 2002

Date and Mint Mark	Description	Buying Price
1952-2002	Jubilee	2.00

2006 Lucky Loonie

ELIZABETH II, MATURE PORTRAIT, 2003 - 2006

Date and Mint Mark	Description	Buying Price
2003	Loon	1.00
2004	Loon	1.00
2004	Lucky Loonie	1.00
2005	Loon	1.00
2005	Terry Fox	1.00
2006	Lucky Loonie	1.00

TWO DOLLAR COINS

ELIZABETH II, DIADEMED PORTRAIT 1996 - 1998

Date and Mint Mark	Description	Buying Price
1996	Polar Bear	2.00
1997	Polar Bear	2.00
1998	Polar Bear	2.00

ELIZABETH II, DIADEMED PORTRAIT, 2001 - 2003

Date and Mint Mark	Description	Buying Price
2001	Polar Bear	2.00
1952-2002	Double Date	2.00
2003	Polar Bear	2.00

ELIZABETH II, DIADEMED PORTRAIT, 1999

Date and Mint Mark	Description	Buying Price
1999	Nunavut	2.00

ELIZABETH II, MATURE PORTRAIT, 2003 - 2006

Date and Mint Mark	Description	Buying Price
2003	Polar Bear	2.00
2004	Polar Bear	2.00
2005	Polar Bear	2.00
2006	Polar Bear	2.00

ELIZABETH II, DIADEMED PORTRAIT, 2000

Date and Mint Mark	Description	Buying Price
2000	Polar Bears	2.00

CIRCULATING GOLD COINS

SOVEREIGNS

EDWARD VII 1908 - 1910

Date and Mint Mark	Buying VF Price
1908C	1,200.00
1909C	225.00
1910C	225.00

FIVE DOLLARS

GEORGE V 1912 - 1914

Date and Mint Mark	Buying VF Price
1912	175.00
1913	175.00
1914	250.00

TEN DOLLARS

GEORGE V 1911 - 1919

Date and Mint Mark	Buying VF Price
1911C	165.00
1913C	400.00
1914C	250.00
1916C	10,000.00
1917C	165.00
1918C	165.00
1919C	165.00

GEORGE V 1912 - 1914

Date and Mint Mark	Buying VF Price
1912	350.00
1913	350.00
1914	375.00

IMPORTANT: Do not clean your coins. Coins should be handled carefully. Only experts should consider cleaning. If you are not an expert, the results can be disastrous.

COLLECTORS ISSUES

The numismatic department of the Royal Canadian Mint issued specially struck and packaged coins starting in 1954. The coins were issued for collectors and as a result are of high quality. The dealer buying prices listed below are for single coins and sets in their original packaging and condition. Coins or sets which have been mishandled or damaged are discounted from the prices listed. Beginning in 1971 the numismatic department of the Royal Canadian Mint issued silver dollars for collectors in two conditions, proof and uncirculated. Proof condition dollars were issued in black leatherette boxes while uncirculated dollars were issued in a clear plastic container.

ONE CENT

Date	Description	Buying Price
2003	Selectively gold plated	10.00

SILVER THREE CENTS

Date	Description	Buying Price
2001	3 Cent Beaver	10.00

SILVER FIVE CENTS

2000-2002 Common Obv.   Les Voltigeurs de Québec

Royal Military College of Canada   85th Anniv. Battle for Vimy Ridge

Date	Description	Buying Price
2000	Les Voltigeurs de Québec	5.00
2001	Royal Military College, Canada	5.00
2002	85th Anniversary, Vimy Ridge	7.00

60th Anniversary D-Day 1944-2004

60th Anniversary VE-Day 1945-2005

1945-2005 Selectively gold platead

Date	Description	Buying Price
2004	60th Anniv. D-Day	30.00
2005	60th Anniv. VE-Day	10.00
2006	1945-2005 Gold plated	10.00

SILVER TEN CENTS

Caboto

Date	Description	Buying Price
1997	Caboto	10.00

100th Anniv. Credit Unions in N.A. 2000

Year of the Volunteers, 2001

Canadian Open Golf, 2004

Date	Description	Buying Price
2000	100th Anniv. Credit Unions	4.00
2001	Int'l Year of Volunteers	5.00
2004	Canadian Open Golf	5.00

TWENTY-FIVE CENTS
125TH ANNIVERSARY 1867-1992

For the complete 12-coin set of the 1867-1992, 125th Anniversary see pages 24 and 25. The set was minted in both nickel and silver

January - New Brunswick

Date	Description	No. of Coins	Buying Price
1992	125th Anniversary silver proof set	13	50.00
1992	Single silver coin	1	4.00
1992	125 Anniversary nickel souvenier set	13	5.00

TWENTY-FIVE CENTS
1999 MILLENNIUM SET

For the complete 24-coin set of the 1999-2000 millennium celebration see pages 25 and 26. The coins were issued in both nickel and silver.

January 1999

1999 Millennium Medallion

September 1999 Mule
Obverse has no denomination

November 1999 Mule
Obverse has no denomination

Date	Description	No. of Coins	Buying Price
1999	12 coin set and 1999 medallion		6.00
1999	September, no denomination		50.00
1999	November, no denomination		50.00
1999	Medallion		1.00
1999	12 coin silver set		50.00
1999	Single silver coin		4.00

TWENTY-FIVE CENTS

2000 MILLENNIUM

January 2000, for complete set see page 26.

2000 Millennium Medallion

2000 Mule
Coin Obverse with Medallion Obverse

Date	Description	Buying Price
2000	12-coin, medallion	8.00
2000	Medallion	2.00
2000	Coin; medallion mule	300.00
2000	12-coin silver set	50.00
2000	Single silver coin	4.00

CANADA'S FIRST COLOURIZED COIN

Date	Description	Buying Price
2000	January	5.00

CANADA DAY SERIES

Canada Day 2000

Canada Day 2001

Canada Day 2002

Canada Day 2003

Canada Day 2004

Moose, 2004

Canada Day 2005

Canada Day 2006

Date	Description	Buying Price
2000	Canada Day 2000	35.00
2001	Canada Day 2001	5.00
2002	Canada Day 2002	6.00
2003	Canada Day 2003	6.00
2004	Canada Day 2004	6.00
2004	Moose	6.00
2005	Canada Day 2005	6.00
2006	Canada Day 2006	6.00

COLLECTORS SERIES 2004-2006

2004
Poppy

2004
Santa Claus

2005
Christmas Stocking

2006
Liberation

2006
Quebec Winter Carnival

2006
Montreal Canadiens

2006
Ottawa Senators

2006
Toronto Maple Leafs

Date	Description	Buying Price
2004	Poppy, Silver	15.00
2004P	Santa Claus, Coloured	10.00
2005P	Christmas Stocking, Coloured	10.00
2006P	Liberation, Silver	15.00
2006P	Quebec Winter Carnival, Coloured	10.00
2006P	Montreal Canadiens, Coloured	10.00
2006P	Ottawa Senators, Coloured	10.00
2006P	Toronto Maple Leafs, Coloured	10.00

PROOF SILVER FIFTY CENTS
WILD LIFE SERIES

| | Atlantic Puffin | Whooping Crane | | Gray Jays | White Tailed Ptarmigans |

Date	Description	Buying Price	Date	Description	Buying Price
1995	Atlantic Puffins	6.00	1995	Gray Jays	6.00
1995	Whooping Crane	6.00	1995	White Tailed Ptarmigans	6.00

| Moose Calf | Wood Ducklings | Cougar Kittens | Black Bear Cubs |

Date	Description	Buying Price	Date	Description	Buying Price
1996	Moose Calf	10.00	1996	Cougar Kittens	10.00
1996	Wood Ducklings	10.00	1996	Black Bear Cubs	10.00

   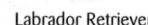

| Newfoundland | Nova Scotia Duck Tolling Retriever | Labrador Retriever | Canadian Eskimo Dog |

Date	Description	Buying Price	Date	Description	Buying Price
1997	Newfoundland	7.00	1997	Labrador Retriever	7.00
1997	Nova Scotia Duck Tolling Retriever	7.00	1997	Canadian Eskimo Dog	7.00

PROOF SILVER FIFTY CENTS
WILD LIFE SERIES

| | Killer Whale | Humpback Whale | | Beluga Whale | Blue Whale |

Date	Description	Buying Price	Date	Description	Buying Price
1998	Killer Whale	7.00	1998	Beluga Whale	7.00
1998	Humpback Whale	7.00	1998	Blue Whale	7.00

| | Tonkinese | Lynx | Cymric | Cougar |

Date	Description	Buying Price	Date	Description	Buying Price
1999	Tonkinese	12.00	1999	Cymric	12.00
1999	Lynx	12.00	1999	Cougar	12.00

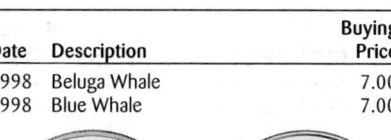 

| | Bald Eagle | Osprey | Great Horned Owl | Red-Tailed Hawk |

Date	Description	Buying Price	Date	Description	Buying Price
2000	Bald Eagle	7.00	2000	Great Horned Owl	7.00
2000	Osprey	7.00	2000	Red-Tailed Hawk	7.00

PROOF SILVER FIFTY CENTS
SPORTS SERIES

| | Skating | | Skiing | | Soccer | | Auto Racing |

Date	Description	Buying Price	Date	Description	Buying Price
1998	Skating	6.00	1998	Soccer	6.00
1998	Skiing	6.00	1998	Auto Racing	6.00

| | Golf | | Yacht Race | | Football | | Basketball |

Date	Description	Buying Price	Date	Description	Buying Price
1999	Golf	8.00	1999	Football	6.00
1999	Yacht Race	6.00	1999	Basketball	6.00

  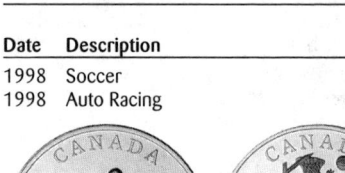 

| | Hockey | | Curling | | Steeplechase | | Bowling |

Date	Description	Buying Price	Date	Description	Buying Price
2000	Hockey	7.00	2000	Steeplechase	6.00
2000	Curling	6.00	2000	Bowling	6.00

PROOF SILVER FIFTY CENTS
CANADIAN FESTIVALS SERIES

Quebec Winter Carnival (Quebec)   Toonik Tyme (Nunavut)   Newfoundland and Labrador Folk Festival (Newfoundland)   Festival of Fathers (Prince Edward Island)

Annapolis Valley Blossom Festival (Nova Scotia)   Stratford Festival of Canada (Ontario)   Folklorama (Manitoba)   Calgary Stampede (Alberta)

Squamish Days Logger Sports (British Columbia)   Yukon Festival (Yukon)   Back to Batoche (Saskatchewan)   Great Northern Arts Festival (Northwest Territories)

Festival Acadien de Caraquet (New Brunswick)

Date	Description	Price	Date	Description	Price
2001	Québec	10.00	2002	Alberta	10.00
2001	Nunavut	10.00	2002	British Columbia	10.00
2001	Newfoundland	10.00	2003	Yukon	10.00
2001	Prince Edward Island	10.00	2003	Saskatchewan	10.00
2002	Nova Scotia	10.00	2003	Northwest Territories	10.00
2002	Ontario	10.00	2003	New Brunswick	10.00
2002	Manitoba	10.00	2001-03	Set Can. Festivals (13 coins)	120.00

PROOF SILVER FIFTY CENTS
CANADIAN FOLKLORE AND LEGENDS SERIES

The Sled

The Maiden's Cave

Les Petits Sauteux

The Pig That Wouldn't

Shoemaker in Heaven

Le Vaisseau Fantome

Date	Description	Price	Date	Description	Price
2001	The Sled	10.00	2002	The Pig That Wouldn't	10.00
2001	The Maiden's Cave	10.00	2002	Shoemaker in Heaven	10.00
2001	Les Petits Sauteux	10.00	2002	Le Vaisseau Fantome	10.00

FLOWER SERIES

Golden Tulip

Golden Daffodil

Golden Lily

Golden Rose

Golden Daisy

Date	Description	Price	Date	Description	Price
2002	Golden Tulip	40.00	2005	Golden Rose	15.00
2003	Golden Dafoodil	20.00	2006	Golden Daisy	15.00
2004	Golden Lily	20.00			

PROOF SILVER FIFTY CENTS
COAT OF ARMS OF CANADA

Kruger-Gray 1953   Shingles 1954-1958   Shingles 1959-1996   Bursey-Sabourin 1997-2005

Date	Description	Buying Price	Date	Description	Buying Price
2004	Kruger-Gray, 1953	10.00	2004	Shingles 1959-1996	10.00
2004	Shingles, 1954-1958	10.00	2004	Bursey-Sabourin, 1997-2005	10.00

CANADIAN BUTTERFLY COLLECTION

Canadian Tiger Swallowtail   Canadian Clouded Sulpher   Monarch

Spangled Fritillary   Short-tailed Swallowtail

Date	Description	Buying Price	Date	Description	Buying Price
2003	Canadian Tiger Swallowtail	15.00	2005	Spangled Fritillary	15.00
2004	Canadian Clouded Sulpher	15.00	2006	Short-tailed Swallowtail	15.00
2005	Monarch	15.00			

QUEST FOR PEACE AND FREEDOM DURING SECOND WORLD WAR

Battle of Britain

Liberation of Netherlands

Conquest of Sicily

Battle of the Scheldt

Raid on Dieppe

Battle of the Atlantic

Date	Description	Buying Price	Date	Description	Buying Price
2005	Battle of Britain	15.00	2005	Battle of the Scheldt	15.00
2005	Liberation of Netherlands	15.00	2005	Raid on Dieppe	15.00
2005	Conquest of Sicily	15.00	2005	Battle of the Atlantic	15.00

HOCKEY LEGENDS

Jean Beliveau

Guy Lafleur

Jacques Plante

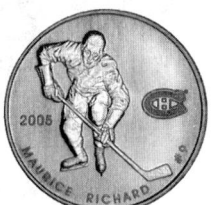
Maurice Richard

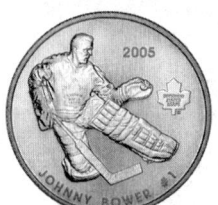
Johnny Bower

Tim Horton

Darryl Sittler

Dave Keon

Date	Description	Buying Price	Date	Description	Buying Price
2005	Jean Beliveau	15.00	2005	Johnny Bower	15.00
2005	Guy Lafleur	15.00	2005	Tim Horton	15.00
2005	Jacques Plante	15.00	2005	Darryl Sittler	15.00
2005	Maurice Richard	15.00	2005	Dave Keon	15.00

SILVER PROOF-LIKE DOLLARS

Single dollars, in either cellophane or pliofilm packaging, were issued by the Royal Canadian Mint for collectors. Illustrations of these dollars can be found on page 32.

Date	Description	Buying Price	Date	Description	Buying Price
1954	Voyageur	150.00	1959	Voyageur	10.00
1955	Voyageur	100.00	1960	Voyageur	10.00
1955	Arnprior	150.00	1961	Voyageur	8.00
1956	Voyageur	60.00	1962	Voyageur	8.00
1957	Voyageur	30.00	1963	Voyageur	8.00
1958	British Columbia	25.00	1964	Charlottetown	8.00

CASED NICKEL DOLLARS

1970 Manitoba

1971 British Columbia

1973 Prince Edward Island

1974 Winnipeg

1982 Constitution

1984 Jacques Cartier

Date	Description	Buying Price	Date	Description	Buying Price
1970	Manitoba	1.00	1975	Voyageur	1.00
1971	British Columbia	1.00	1976	Voyageur	1.00
1972	Voyageur	1.00	1982	Constitution	2.00
1973	Prince Edward Island	1.00	1984	Jacques Cartier	2.00
1974	Winnipeg	1.00			

CASED SILVER DOLLARS

Common Obverse

1971 British Columbia

1973 R.C.M.P.

1974 Winnipeg Centennial

1975 Calgary

1976 Library of Parliament

1977 Silver Jubilee

1978 Commonwealth Games

1979 Griffon Tricentennial

Date	Description	Buying Price
1971	British Columbia Centennial	4.00
1972	Voyageur	4.00
1973	R.C.M.P.	4.00
1974	Winnipeg Centennial	4.00
1975	Calgary Stampede	4.00

Date	Description	Buying Price
1976	Library of Parliament	4.00
1977	Silver Jubilee	4.00
1978	Commonwealth Games	4.00
1979	Griffon Tricentennial	4.00

CASED SILVER DOLLARS

1980 Arctic Territories

1981 Trans-Canada Railway

1982 Regina Centennial

1983 World University Games

1984 Toronto Sesquicentennial

1985 National Parks Centannial

1986 Vancouver Centennial

1987 John Davis Strait

1988 Saint-Maurice Ironworks

Date	Description	Buying Price	Date	Description	Buying Price
1980	Arctic Territories Centennial	6.00	1985	National Parks Centennial (PR)	4.00
1981	Trans-Canada Railway (PR)	4.00	1985	National Parks Centennial (UNC)	4.00
1981	Trans-Canada Railway (UNC)	4.00	1986	Vancouver Centennial (PR)	4.00
1982	Regina Centennial (PR)	4.00	1986	Vancouver Centennial (UNC)	4.00
1982	Regina Centennial (UNC)	4.00	1987	Davis Strait (PR)	4.00
1983	World University Games (PR)	4.00	1987	Davis Strait (UNC)	4.00
1983	World University Games (UNC)	4.00	1988	Sainte-Maurice Ironworks (PR)	6.00
1984	Toronto Sesquicentennial (PR)	4.00	1988	Sainte-Maurice Ironworks (UNC)	4.00
1984	Toronto Sesquicentennial (UNC)	4.00			

CASED SILVER DOLLARS

1989 MacKenzie River   Common Obverse 1990 - 2003   1990 Henry Kelsey Tricentennial

  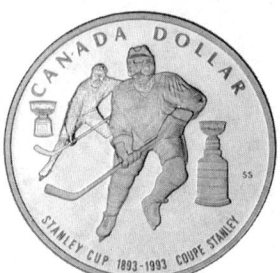

1991 Frontenac   1992 Kingston Stagecoach   1993 Stanley Cup

1994 R.C.M.P. Northern Dog Team Patrol   1995 325th Anniv. Founding of Hudson's Bay Co.   1996 200th Anniversary John McIntosh

Date	Description	Buying Price	Date	Description	Buying Price
1989	MacKenzie River (PR)	6.00	1993	Stanley Cup (PR)	6.00
1989	MacKenzie River (UNC)	4.00	1993	Stanley Cup (UNC)	4.00
1990	Henry Kelsey (PR)	6.00	1994	R.C.M.P. (PR)	10.00
1990	Henry Kelsey (UNC)	4.00	1994	R.C.M.P. (UNC)	5.50
1991	Frontenac (PR)	10.00	1995	Hudson's Bay (PR)	10.00
1991	Frontenac (UNC)	4.00	1995	Hudson's Bay (UNC)	6.00
1992	Kingston Stagecoach (PR)	6.00	1996	McIntosh (PR)	10.00
1992	Kingston Stagecoach (UNC)	4.00	1996	McIntosh (UNC)	6.00

CASED SILVER DOLLARS

1997 Canada/Russia Hockey

1997 Flying Loon

1998 125th Anniversary RCMP

1999 225th Anniv. Juan Perez

1999 Int'l Year Older Persons

2000 Voyage of Discovery

2001 50th Anniversary National Ballet of Canada

2001 90th Anniversary Canada's 1911 Silver Dollar

2002 50th Anniv. Elizabeth II's Accession to the Throne

Date	Description	Buying Price
1997	Hockey (PR)	10.00
1997	Hockey (UNC)	5.50
1997	Flying Loon (PR)	60.00
1998	RCMP (PR)	10.00
1998	RCMP (UNC)	6.00
1999	Perez (PR)	10.00
1999	Perez (UNC)	6.00
1999	Older Persons (PR)	20.00

Date	Description	Buying Price
2000	Voyage of Discovery (PR)	10.00
2000	Voyage of Discovery (UNC)	6.00
2001	National Ballet of Canada (PR)	10.00
2001	National Ballet of Canada (UNC)	6.00
2001	90th Anniv. 1911 Silver Dollar (PR)	12.00
2002	50th Anniv. Accession (PR)	10.00
2002	50th Anniv. Accession (UNC)	6.00

Note: **(PR)** Proof condition one dollar silver coins are issued in a black leatherette case.
(UNC) UNC condition one dollar silver coins are issued in a clear plastic case.

CASED SILVER DOLLARS

2002 Queen Mother · 2003 Cobalt · Common Obv. 2003 to date

2003 50th Anniv. Coronation · 2004 First French Settlement · 2004 The Poppy

2005 40th Anniv. Canadian Flag · 2006 150th Anniv. Victoria Cross

Date	Description	Buying Price
2002	Queen Mother (PR)	150.00
2003	Cobalt (PR)	10.00
2003	Cobalt (Unc)	6.00
2003	Coronation (PR)	15.00
2004	First French Settlement	15.00
2004	First French Settlement (Unc)	6.00

Date	Description	Buying Price
2004	Lucky Loon (PR)	20.00
2004	The Poppy (PR)	15.00
2005	40th Anniv. Can. Flag (PR)	20.00
2005	40th Anniv. Can. Flag (Unc)	10.00
2005	40th Anniv. Can. Flag (enam.)	100.00
2006	Victoria Cross (PR)	25.00
2006	Victoria Cross (Unc)	12.00

SILVER LOON DOLLARS

Common Obv. 2004-2006   2004 Lucky Loonie   2006 Lucky Loonie   2006 Lullabies Loonie

Date	Description	Buying Price	Date	Description	Buying Price
2004	Lucky Loonie	20.00	2006	Lullabies Loonie	20.00
2006	Lucky Loonie	20.00			

BRONZE DOLLARS

Common obv. 1992-1997   1992 125th Anniv.   1994 Remembrance   1995 Peacekeeping

1997 Flying Loon   2002 Family of Loons   2002 Centre Ice   Common obv. 2004-2006

2004 Canada Goose   2004 Elusive Loon   2005 Puffin   2006 Snowy Owl

Date	Description	Buying Price	Date	Description	Buying Price
1992	125th Anniv. of Canada	2.00	2002	Centre Ice	20.00
1994	Remembrance	2.00	2004	Canada Goose	15.00
1995	Peacekeeping	2.00	2005	Elusive Loon	10.00
1997	Flying Loon	50.00	2005	Tufted Puffin	10.00
2002	Family of Loons	20.00	2006	Snowy Owl	10.00

TWO DOLLARS

1996 Polar Bear   2000 Polar Bears

ELIZABETH II 1996

Date	Description	Buying Price
1996	Proof	5.00
1996	Piedfort	30.00
1996	Gold	75.00

ELIZABETH II 2000

Date	Description	Buying Price
2000	Proof	6.00
2000	Silver	15.00
2000	Gold	75.00

1999 Nunavut - Ring   2004 Polar Bear, Silver

ELIZABETH II 2004

Date	Description	Buying Price
2004	Polar Bear, Silver	20.00

1999 Nunavut - No Ring

2006 Gold

ELIZABETH II 1999

Date	Description	Buying Price
1999	Silver	10.00
1999	Gold	75.00
1999	Mule, No Ring	50.00

ELIZABETH II 2006

Date	Description	Buying Price
2006	10th Anniv. Gold Two Dollar	100.00

FIVE DOLLAR COINS

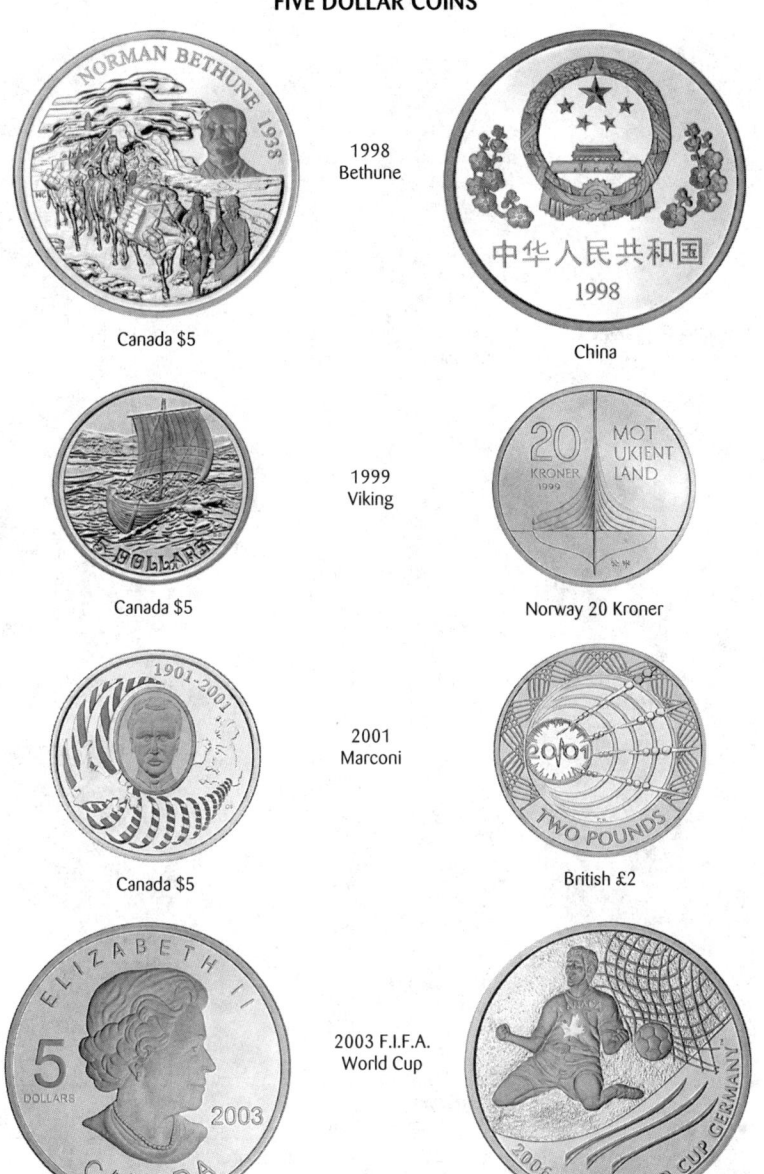

1998 Bethune

Canada $5 — China

1999 Viking

Canada $5 — Norway 20 Kroner

2001 Marconi

Canada $5 — British £2

2003 F.I.F.A. World Cup

Date	Description	Buying Price
1998	Bethune, 2 coin set	20.00
1999	Viking Settlement, 2 coin set	20.00
2001	Marconi, 2 coin set	30.00
2004	World Cup	30.00

FIVE DOLLAR COINS

Common obv. (except for date) 2004-2005

2004 100th Anniversary Canadian Open Championship

2004 Majestic Moose

2005 60th Anniversary of the end of the Second World War

Common obv. 2005-2006

2005 Alberta Centennial

2005 Saskatchewan Centennial

Obverse 2006

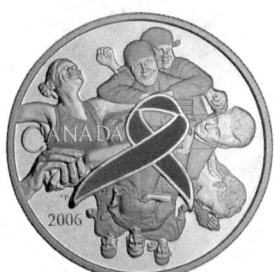
2006 Breast Cancer

Date	Description	Buying Price
2004	100th Anniv. Canadian Open Golf	15.00
2004	Majestic Moose	35.00
2005	60th Anniv., RCM Rev.	15.00
2005	60th Anniv., BRM Rev.; Privy Mark	15.00

Date	Description	Buying Price
2005	Alberta Centennial	15.00
2005	Saskatchewan Centennial	15.00
2006	Breast Cancer	15.00

FIVE DOLLAR COIN

Common obv. 2005-2006

2005 White-tailed Deer and Fawn

2005 Atlantic Walrus and Calf

2006 Peregrine Falcon and Nestlings

2006 Sable Island Horse and Foal

Photograph not available at press time

Snowbirds

Date	Description	Buying Price
2005	White-tailed Deer and Fawn	15.00
2005	Atlantic Walrus and Calf	15.00
2006	Peregrine Falcon and Nestlings	15.00

Date	Description	Buying Price
2006	Sable Island Horse and Foal	15.00
2006	Snowbirds	15.00

FIVE AND TEN DOLLAR COINS
1976 MONTREAL OLYMPIC COINS

For the Summer Olympic Games of 1976, held in Montreal, seven series of silver coins were minted. There were four different coins in each series. Two $5.00 and two $10.00 coins, struck in sterling silver. The $5.00 coins weigh 24.3 grams and the $10.00 coins weigh 48.6 grams. The coins were available, encapsulated in plastic, as single coins, and in custom, prestige and proof four-coin sets. Each set of four coins, with a face value of $30.00, contains 4.28 oz. of fine silver. The purchase price of these sets is linked to the market price of silver, even if the intrinsic value falls below the face value. Large quantities of these coins were issued, and they are not redeemable by the government or the banks.

SERIES I

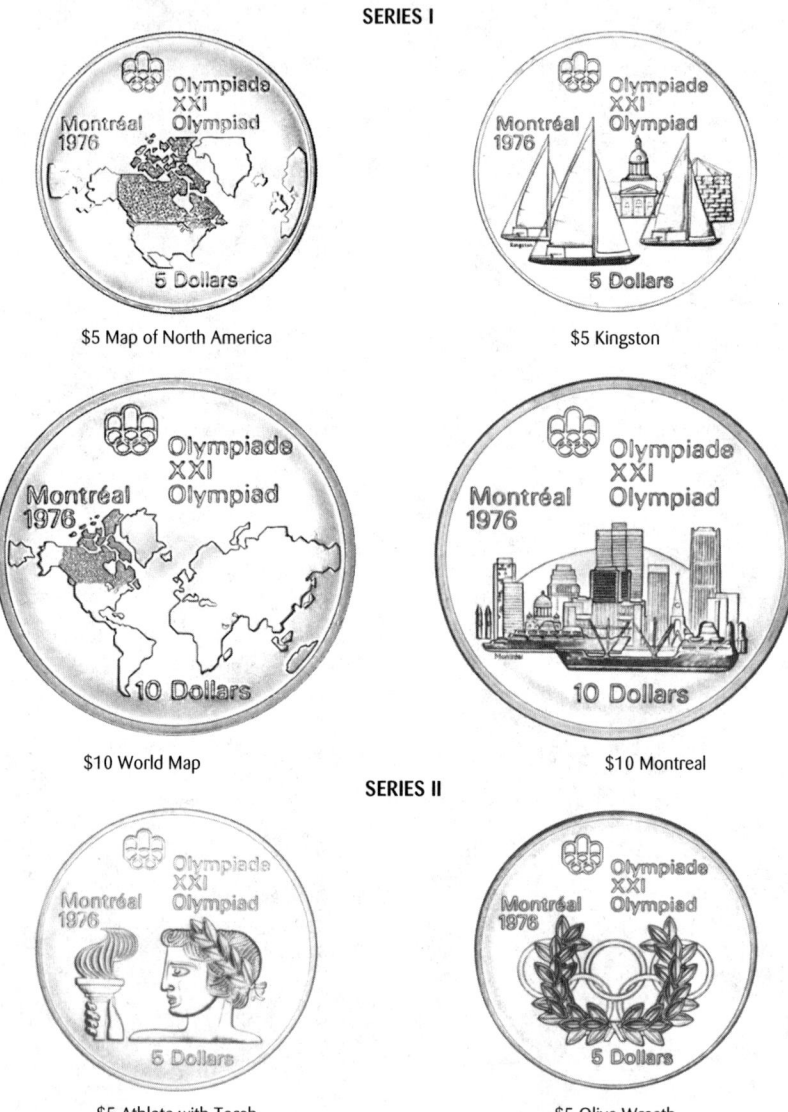

$5 Map of North America

$5 Kingston

$10 World Map

$10 Montreal

SERIES II

$5 Athlete with Torch

$5 Olive Wreath

FIVE AND TEN DOLLAR COINS

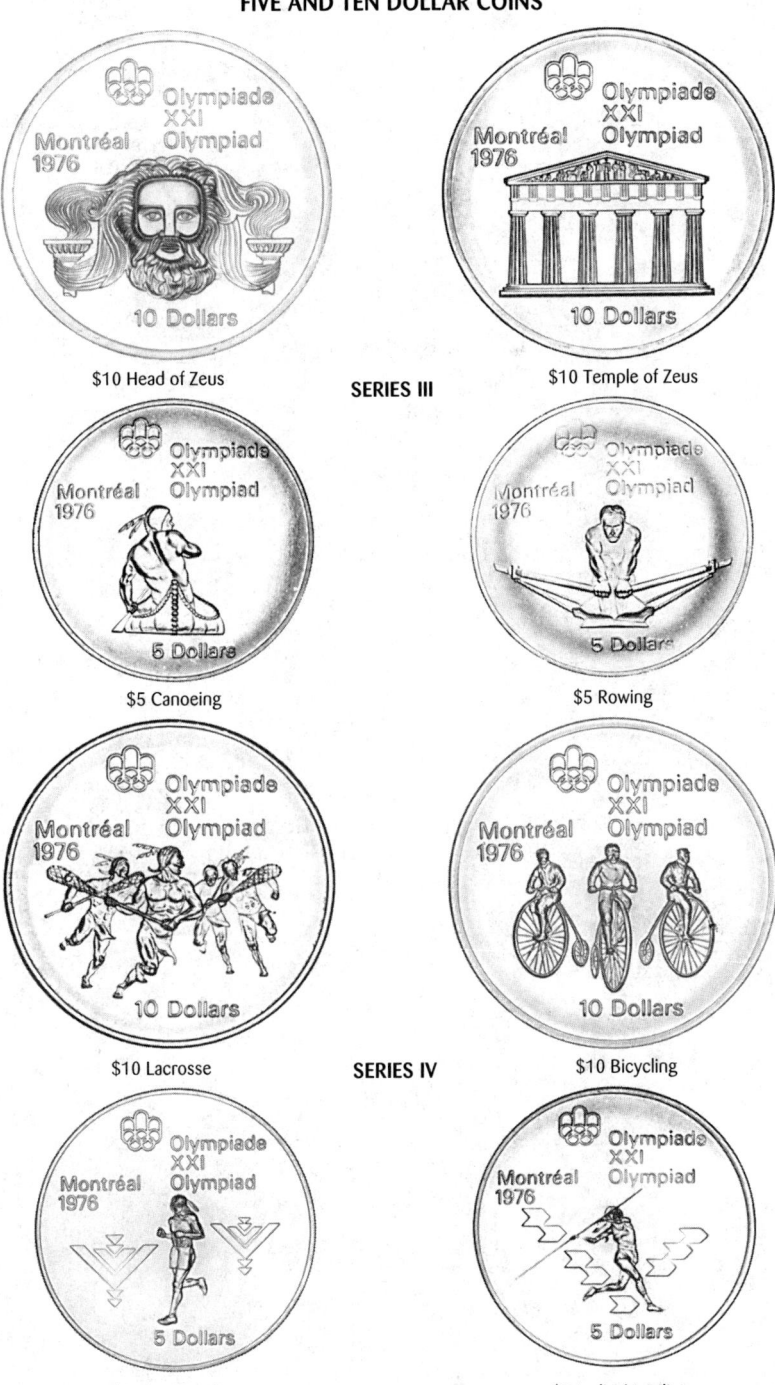

$10 Head of Zeus — SERIES III — $10 Temple of Zeus

$5 Canoeing — $5 Rowing

$10 Lacrosse — SERIES IV — $10 Bicycling

$5 The Marathon — $5 Ladies' Javelin

FIVE AND TEN DOLLAR COINS

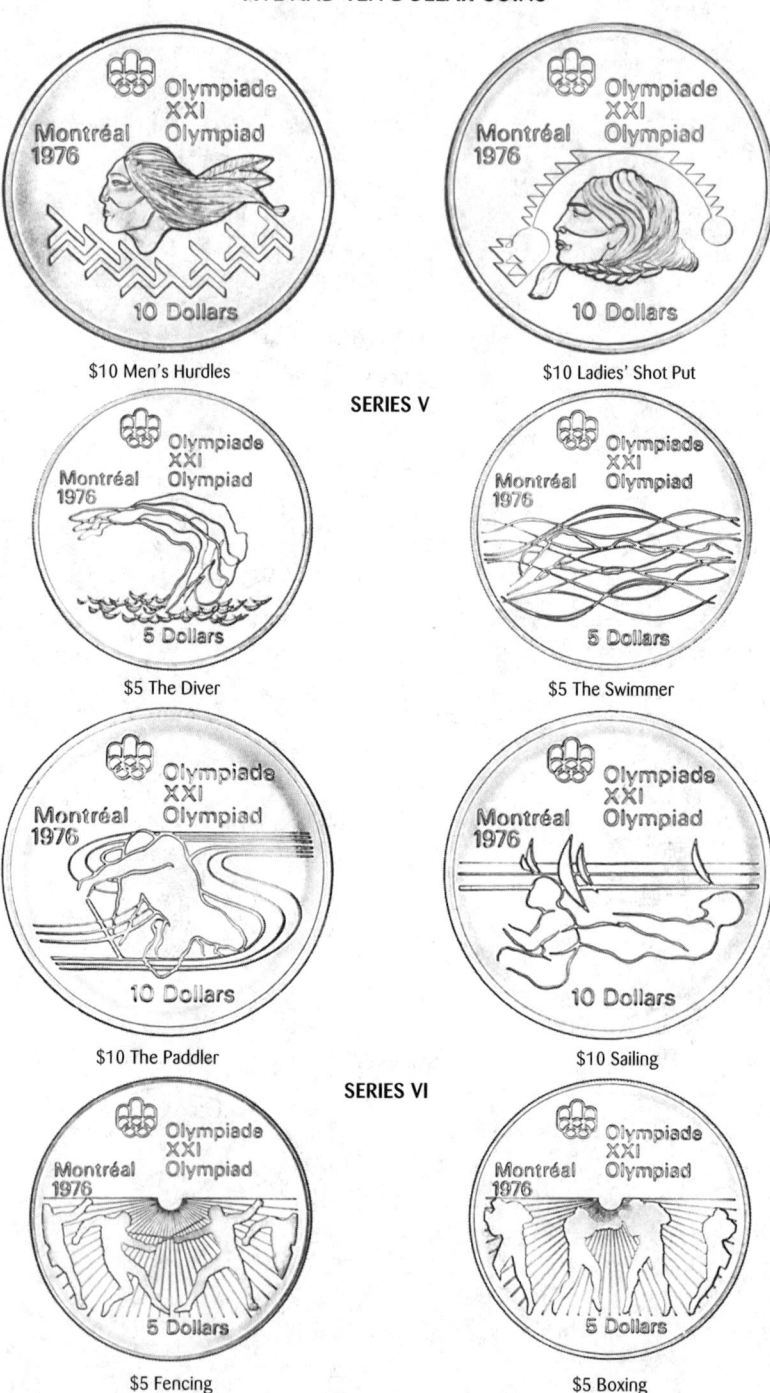

$10 Men's Hurdles $10 Ladies' Shot Put

SERIES V

$5 The Diver $5 The Swimmer

$10 The Paddler $10 Sailing

SERIES VI

$5 Fencing $5 Boxing

FIVE AND TEN DOLLAR COINS

$10 Field Hockey

$10 Football

SERIES VII

$5 Olympic Flame

$5 Oylmpic Village

$10 Olympic Stadium

$10 Olympic Velodrome

Date	Series	$5 Coin	$10 Coin	Custom Set	Prestige Set	Proof Set
1973	1	7.00	14.00	62.00	62.00	65.00
1974	Mule	–	150.00	–	–	–
1974	2	7.00	14.00	62.00	62.00	65.00
1974	3	7.00	14.00	62.00	62.00	65.00
1975	4	7.00	14.00	62.00	62.00	65.00
1975	5	7.00	14.00	62.00	62.00	65.00
1976	6	7.00	14.00	62.00	62.00	65.00
1976	7	7.00	14.00	62.00	62.00	65.00

EIGHT DOLLAR COINS

2004 Obv.

2004 Great Grizzly

2005 Railway Bridge

Elizabeth II 2004-2005

2005 Chinese Memorial

Date	Description	Buying Price	Date	Description	Buying Price
2004	Great Grizzly	25.00	2005	Chinese Memorial	25.00
2005	Railway Bridge	25.00			

TEN DOLLAR COINS

2005 Year of the Veteran

2006 Pope John Paul II

2006 Fortress of Louisbourg

Date	Description	Buying Price	Date	Description	Buying Price
2005	Year of the Veteran	25.00	2006	Fortress of Louisbourg	25.00
2006	Pope John Paul II	25.00			

FIFTEEN DOLLAR COINS
Olympic Centennial Coins

Olympic Sports Reverse
Speed Skater, Pole Vaulter, Gymnast

Olympic Spirit Reverse

Date	Description	Buying Price	Date	Description	Buying Price
1992	Sports	15.00	1992	Spirit of the Generations	15.00

FIFTEEN DOLLAR COINS
Chinese Lunar Calender Coins

1998 The Year of the Tiger

1999 The Year of the Rabbit

2000 The Year of the Dragon

2001 The Year of the Snake

2002 The Year of the Horse

2003 The Year of the Ram

2004 The Year of the Monkey

2005 The Year of the Rooster

2006 Year of the Dog

Date	Description	Buying Price	Date	Description	Buying Price
1998	Tiger	250.00	2003	Ram	40.00
1999	Rabbit	25.00	2004	Monkey	40.00
2000	Dragon	85.00	2005	Rooster	40.00
2001	Snake	30.00	2006	Dog	40.00
2002	Horse	40.00			

TWENTY DOLLAR COINS
CALGARY OLYMPIC GAMES

The XV Winter Olympic Games were held in Calgary, February 13th to 29th, 1988. Ten different $20 silver coins were issued to commemorate this event. The coins weigh 34.107 grams, the composition is .925 silver and .075 copper, and they were issued in proof singles or proof sets in one or two coin display cases. Incorporated into the design of these coins are the letters "XV OLYMPIC WINTER GAMES - XVes JEUX OLYMPIQUE D'HIVER" impressed into the edge. During the striking of these coins at the Royal Canadian Mint, the impressed procedures were skipped on some series resulting in the edge lettering being missed on four known coins, resulting in varieties.

FIRST SERIES

Downhill Skiing

Speed Skating

SECOND SERIES

Hockey

Biathalon

THIRD SERIES

Cross-Country Skiing

Free-Style Skiing

TWENTY DOLLAR COINS

FOURTH SERIES

Figure Skating

Curling

FIFTH SERIES

Ski Jumping

Bobsleigh

Date	Description	Buying Single	Buying Set
1985	Downhill Skiiing	20.00	
1985	Speed Skating	20.00	40.00
1985	Speed Skating, no edge lettering	100.00	
1986	Hockey	20.00	
1986	Hockey, no edge lettering	100.00	
1986	Biathalon	20.00	40.00
1986	Biathalon, no edge lettering	100.00	
1986	Cross-Country Skiing	20.00	
1986	Free-Style Skiing	20.00	40.00
1986	Free-Style Skiing, no edge lettering	100.00	
1987	Figure Skating	20.00	
1987	Curling	20.00	40.00
1987	Ski Jumping	20.00	
1987	Bobsleigh	20.00	40.00

TWENTY DOLLAR COINS

AVIATION FIRST SERIES 1990 - 1994

Canada's aviation heroes and their achievements are commemorated on this first series of twenty dollar sterling-silver coins. The series is made up of ten coins, which were issued two per year over five years. For the first time, each coin design contains a 24-karat-gold-covered oval cameo portrait of the aviation hero commemorated. A maximum of 50,000 of each coin was offered for sale.

Coin No. 1
Anson and Harvard /
Robert Leckie

Coin No. 2
Avro Lancaster /
J. E. Fauquier

Coin No. 3
A. E. A. Silver Dart / F. W. Baldwin
and J. A. D. McCurdy

Coin No. 4
de Havilland Beaver /
Phillip C. Garratt

Coin No. 5
Curtiss JN-4 (Canuck) /
Sir F. W. Baillie

Coin No. 6
de Havilland Gypsy Moth /
Murton A. Seymour

TWENTY DOLLAR COINS

AVIATION FIRST SERIES 1990 - 1994 (cont.)

Coin No. 7
Fairchild 71C / J. A. Richardson

Coin No. 8
Super Electra / Z. L. Leigh

Coin No. 9
Curtiss HS-2L / Stuart Graham

Coin No. 10
Vickers Vedette / T. Reid

Date	Coin No.	Description	Buying Price
1990	1	Anson and Harvard / Leckie	25.00
1990	2	Lancaster / Fauquier	60.00
1991	3	Silver Dart / Baldwin, McCurdy	20.00
1991	4	Beaver / Garratt	20.00
1992	5	Curtiss / Baille	20.00
1992	6	Gypsy Moth / Seymour	20.00
1993	7	Fairchild / Richardson	20.00
1993	8	Super Electra / Leigh	20.00
1994	9	Curtiss / Graham	20.00
1994	10	Vedette / Reid	20.00

TWENTY DOLLAR COINS

AVIATION SECOND SERIES 1995 - 1999

This second series of aviation coins celebrates "Powered Flight in Canada – Beyond World War II." As with the first series, it was made up of ten coins to be issued two per year over five years. Each coin design contains a 24-karat-gold-covered oval cameo portrait of the pilot, engineers or designers of the aircrafts. A maximum of 50,000 of each coin was offered for sale.

Coin No. 11
The Fleet 80 Canuck / Noury

Coin No. 12
DHC-1 Chipmunk / Bannock

Coin No. 13
CF-100 Canuck / Zurakowski

Coin No. 14
CF-105 Arrow / Chamberlain

Date	Coin No.	Description	Buying Price
1995	11	Fleet 80 Canuck / Noury	20.00
1995	12	DHC-1 Chipmunk / Bannock	20.00
1996	13	CF-100 Canuck / Zurakowski	20.00
1996	14	CF-105 Arrow / Chamberlin	50.00

TWENTY DOLLAR COINS

AVIATION SECOND SERIES 1995 - 1999 (cont.)

Coin No. 15
Canadian F-86 Sabre /
Fern Villeneuve

Coin No. 16
Canadair CT-114 Tutor /
Edward Higgins

Coin No. 17
CP-107 Argus /
William S. Longhurst

Coin No. 18
CL-215 Waterbomber /
Paul Gagnon

Coin No. 19
DHC-6 Twin Otter / G. A. Neal

Coin No. 20
DHC-8 Dash 8 / R. H. Fowler

Date	Coin No.	Description	Buying Price
1997	15	F-86 Sabre / Villeneuve	20.00
1997	16	CT-114 Tutor / Higgin	20.00
1998	17	CP-107 Argus / Longhurst	20.00
1998	18	CL-215 Waterbomber / Gagnon	20.00
1999	19	DHC-6 Twin Otter / Neal	30.00
1999	20	DHC-8 Dash 8 / Fowler	30.00

TWENTY DOLLAR COINS

LAND, SEA AND RAIL 2000 - 2002

Coin No. 1
H. S. Taylor Steam Buggy

Coin No. 2
The Bluenose

Coin No. 3
The Toronto

Coin No. 4
The Russel

Coin No. 5
The Marco Polo

Coin No. 6
The Scotia

Coin No. 7
The Gray-Dort

Coin No. 8
The William Lawrence

Coin No. 9
The D-10 Locomotive

Date	Coin No.	Description	Buying Price
2000	1	H. S. Taylor Steam Buggy	35.00
2000	2	The Bluenose	100.00
2000	3	The Toronto	30.00
2001	4	The Russel	30.00
2001	5	The Marco Polo	30.00
2001	6	The Scotia	30.00
2002	7	The Gray-Dort	30.00
2002	8	The William Lawrence	30.00
2002	9	The D-10 Locomotive	30.00

TWENTY DOLLAR COINS

LAND, SEA AND RAIL 2003

Coin No. 10
HMCS Bras d'or

Coin No. 11
CNR FA-1 Diesel Electric

Coin No. 12
Bricklin SV-1

Date	Coin No.	Description	Buying Price
2003	10	HMCS Bras d'or	35.00
2003	11	C.N.R. FA-1 Diesel Electric Locomotive	35.00
2003	12	Bricklin SV-1	35.00

NATURAL WONDERS COLLECTION

Coin No. 1 Niagara Falls

Coin No. 2 Rocky Mountains

Coin No. 3 Icebergs

Coin No. 4 Northern Lights

Coin No. 5 Hopewell Rocks

Coin No. 6 Diamonds

Date	Coin No.	Description	Buying Price
2003	1	Niagara Falls	40.00
2003	2	Rocky Mountains	35.00
2004	3	Icebergs	35.00
2004	4	Northern Lights	35.00
2005	5	Hopewell Rocks	35.00
2005	6	Diamonds	35.00

TWENTY DOLLAR COINS

TALL SHIPS COLLECTION

Coin No. 1 Three-Masted Ship

Coin No. 2 Ketch

Date	Coin No.	Description	Buying Price
2005	1	Three-masted Ship	35.00
2006	2	Ketch	35.00

NATIONAL PARKS SERIES

Coin No. 1 North Pacific Rim

Coin No. 2 Mingan Archipelago

Coin No. 3 Georgian Bay

Coin No. 4 Nahanni Park

Date	Coin No.	Description	Buying Price
2005	1	North Pacific Rim National Park Reserve	35.00
2005	2	Mingan Archipelago National Park Reserve	35.00
2006	3	Georgian Bay Islands National Park	35.00
2006	4	Nahanni National Park Reserve	35.00

TWENTY DOLLAR COINS

CANADIAN ARCHITECTURAL COLLECTION

Coin No. 1 Notre Dame Basilica Coin No. 2 CN Tower

Date	Coin No.	Description	Buying Price
2006	1	Notre Dame Basilica	35.00
2006	2	30th Anniversary CN Tower	35.00

THIRTY DOLLAR COINS

Welcome Figure Totem Pole National War Memorial 5th Anniversary Canadarm

Date	Description	Buying Price
2006	Welcome Figure Totem Pole	40.00
2006	National War Memorial	40.00
2006	5th Anniversary Canadarm	40.00

NON CIRCULATING GOLD COINS

TWENTY DOLLAR GOLD COIN

Date	Description	Buying Price
1967	$20 Coin	350.00
1967	7 Coin Set	360.00
1967	Medallion Set	15.00

FIFTY DOLLAR GOLD COIN

Date	Description	Buying Price
2005	60th Anniv. End of Second World War	150.00

SEVENTY FIVE DOLLAR GOLD COIN

Date	Description	Buying Price
2005	Pope John Paul II	300.00

ONE HUNDRED DOLLAR GOLD COINS

Canada issued the first one-hundred-dollar gold coin in 1976 to commemorate the Montreal Olympic Games. In that year two qualities and proportions of fineness were released; uncirculated coins were .585 fine (14 karat), and proof coins were .916 fine (22 karat). From 1976 to 1986, only proof quality coins with a fineness of .916 were issued. In 1987 the quality remained the same (proof), but the fineness of the coin was altered to .583 fine, or 14 karat, again.

IMPORTANT

Proof coins must be in mint-state condition. Mishandled, mounted or damaged coins are discounted from the prices listed. The buying price for gold coins is tied to the market price of gold. Any movement in the gold price will result in a corresponding price movement for these coins.

1976 - 14kt   1976 - 22 kt

1977   1978   1979   1980

1981   1982   1983   1984

Date	Description	Fineness	Buying Price	Date	Description	Fineness	Buying Price
1976	14 kt Olympic	.583	140.00	1980	Arctic Territories	.916	280.00
1976	22 kt Olympic	.916	280.00	1981	"O Canada"	.916	280.00
1977	Jubilee	.916	280.00	1982	Constitution	.916	280.00
1978	Unity	.916	280.00	1983	Gilbert's Landing	.916	280.00
1979	Year of the Child	.916	280.00	1984	Voyage of Discovery	.916	280.00

ONE HUNDRED DOLLAR GOLD COINS

Date	Description	Fineness	Buying Price
1985	National Parks	.916	280.00
1986	Peace	.916	280.00
1987	Calgary Olympics	.583	140.00
1988	Bowhead Whale	.583	140.00
1989	Ste. Marie	.583	140.00
1990	Literacy Year	.583	140.00
1991	Empress of India	.583	140.00
1992	Montreal	.583	140.00
1993	Horseless Carriage	.583	160.00
1994	The Home Front	.583	165.00
1995	Louisbourg	.583	170.00
1996	Klondike Gold Rush	.583	175.00
1997	Bell	.583	175.00
1998	Insulin	.583	175.00
1999	Newfoundland	.583	190.00
2000	Northwest Passage	.583	190.00

ONE HUNDRED DOLLAR GOLD COINS

2001 2002 2003 2004

2005 2006

Date	Description	Fineness	Buying Price	Date	Description	Fineness	Buying Price
2001	Library	.583	190.00	2004	Seaway	.583	200.00
2002	Oil Well	.583	340.00	2005	Supreme Court	.583	200.00
2003	Wheat	.583	240.00	2006	Hockey	.583	200.00

150 DOLLAR GOLD COINS

175 DOLLAR GOLD COIN

2000   2001

Date	Description	Fineness	Buying Price
1992	Olympic	.916	350.00

2002   2003

2004   2005

2006

Date	Description	Fineness	Buying Price
2000	Year of the Dragon	.750	500.00
2001	Year of the Snake	.750	200.00
2002	Year of the Horse	.750	225.00
2003	Year of the Ram	.750	225.00
2004	Year of the Monkey	.750	225.00
2005	Year of the Rooster	.750	225.00
2006	Year of the Dog	.750	225.00

200 DOLLAR GOLD COINS

22 KARAT (.916) GOLD

Date	Description	Buying Price
1990	Canada Flag	280.00
1991	A National Passion	280.00
1992	Niagara Falls	280.00
1993	RCMP	280.00
1994	Anne of Green Gables	280.00
1995	Sugar Bush	280.00
1996	Transcontinental	280.00
1997	Haida	400.00
1998	White Buffalo	280.00

Date	Description	Buying Price
1999	Mikmaq Butterfly	280.00
2000	Mother and Child	300.00
2001	Cornelius Krieghoff	300.00
2002	Tom Thomson	300.00
2003	Lionel Fitzgerald	300.00
2004	Alfred Pellan	300.00
2005	Fur Traders	300.00
2006	Timber Trade	300.00

300 DOLLAR GOLD COINS

14 KARAT (.583) GOLD, LARGE SIZE (50 mm)

2002 Jubilee / Triple Cameo

2003 Great Seal of Canada

2004 Arms of Canada / Quadruple Cameo

2005 Britannia

2006 The 1900 Shinplaster

Images shown smaller than actual size

Date	Description	Buying Price	Date	Description	Buying Price
2002	Jubilee / Triple Cameo Portraits	800.00	2005	Britannia	800.00
2003	Great Seal of Canada	800.00	2006	The 1900 Shinplaster	800.00
2004	Quadruple Cameo Portraits	800.00			

300 DOLLAR GOLD COINS

14 KARAT (.583) GOLD, SMALL SIZE (40 mm)

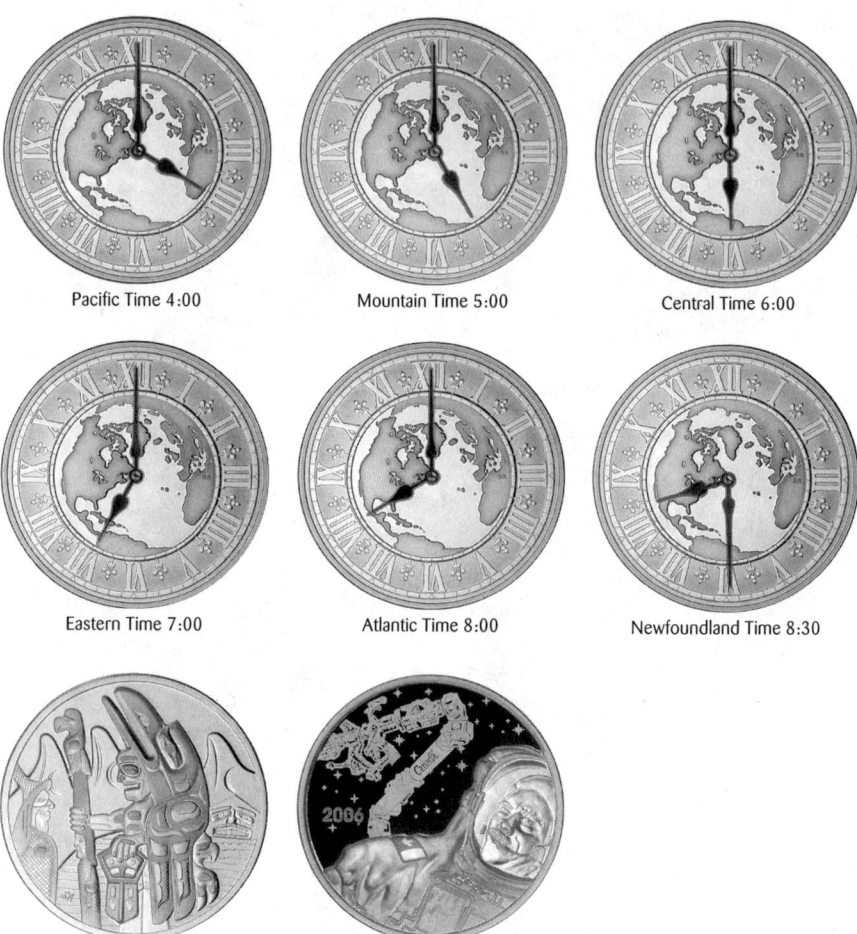

Pacific Time 4:00   Mountain Time 5:00   Central Time 6:00

Eastern Time 7:00   Atlantic Time 8:00   Newfoundland Time 8:30

Welcome Figure Totem Pole   5th Anniv. Canadarm

Date	Description	Buying Price	Date	Description	Buying Price
2005	Pacific Time 4:00	600.00	2005	Atlantic Time 8:00	600.00
2005	Mountain Time 5:00	600.00	2005	Newfoundland Time 8:30	600.00
2005	Central Time 6:00	600.00	2005	Welcome Figure Totem Pole	600.00
2005	Eastern Time 7:00	600.00	2006	5th Anniv. Canadarm	600.00

Note: Images shown smaller than actual size.

350 DOLLAR GOLD COINS
24 Karat (.99999) GOLD

Date	Description	Buying Price
1998	90th Anniv. R.C.M.	850.00
1999	Golden Slipper	850.00
2000	Pacific Dogwood	850.00
2001	Mayflower	850.00
2002	Wild Rose	850.00

Date	Description	Buying Price
2003	Trillium	850.00
2004	Fireweed	850.00
2005	Western Red Lily	850.00
2006	Iris Versicolor	850.00

PROOF PLATINUM COINS

Date	Description	Buying Price	Date	Description	Buying Price
1990	Polar Bear Set	1,950.00	1997	Wood Bison $30	100.00
1991	Snowy Owl Set	1,950.00	1997	Wood Bison $150	500.00
1992	Cougar Set	1,950.00	1998	Grey Wolf Set	1,950.00
1993	Arctic Foxes Set	1,950.00	1998	Grey Wolf $30	100.00
1994	Sea Otters Set	1,950.00	1998	Grey Wolf $150	500.00
1995	Canada Lynx Set	1,950.00	1999	Muskox Set	1,950.00
1995	Canada Lynx $30	100.00	1999	Muskox $30	100.00
1995	Canada Lynx $150	500.00	2000	Pronghorn Set	1,950.00
1996	Peregrine Falcon Set	1,950.00	2001	Harlequin Duck Set	1,950.00
1996	Peregrine Falcon $30	100.00	2002	Great Blue Heron Set	1,950.00
1996	Peregrine Falcon $50	500.00	2003	Atlantic Walrus Set	1,950.00
1997	Wood Bison Set	1,950.00	2004	Grizzly Bear Set	1,950.00

Note: The Platinum Proof Set contains four coins: $300., $150., $75. and $30. coins.

COLLECTOR SETS

Listed on this and the following page are the Collector sets of coins issued by the Royal Canadian Mint between the years 1954 and 2005.

SIX COIN PROOF-LIKE AND BRILLIANT UNCIRCULATED SETS

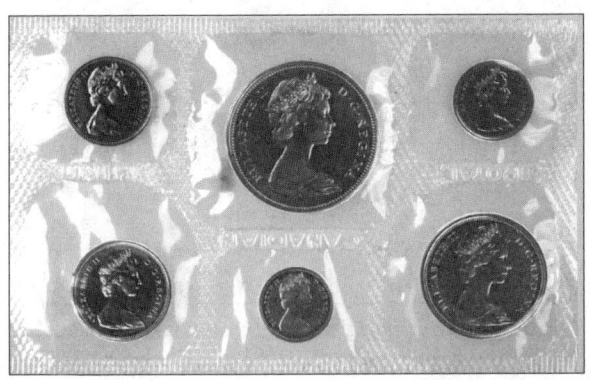

SILVER 6-COIN PROOF-LIKE SETS

Date	Description	Buying Price
1954	Voyageur	275.00
1955	Voyageur	160.00
1955	Arnprior	185.00
1956	Voyageur	90.00
1957	Voyageur	50.00
1958	British Columbia	45.00
1959	Voyageur	20.00
1960	Voyageur	12.00
1961	Voyageur	12.00
1962	Voyageur	12.00
1963	Voyageur	12.00
1964	Charlottetown	12.00
1965	Voyageur	12.00
1966	Voyageur	12.00
1967	Centennial	12.00

NICKEL 6-COIN BRILLIANT UNCIRCULATED SETS

Date	Description	Buying Price
1968	Voyageur	2.00
1969	Voyageur	2.00
1970	Manitoba	2.00
1971	British Columbia	2.00
1972	Voyageur	2.00
1973	R.C.M.P., Small Bust	2.00
1973	R.C.M.P., Large Bust	100.00
1974	Winnipeg	2.00
1975	Voyageur	2.00
1976	Voyageur	2.00
1977	Voyageur	2.00
1978	Voyageur	2.00
1979	Voyageur	2.00
1980	Voyageur	2.00
1981	Voyageur	2.00
1982	Voyageur	2.00
1983	Voyageur	3.00
1984	Voyageur	3.00
1985	Voyageur	3.00
1986	Voyageur	3.00
1987	Voyageur	3.00
1988	Loon	3.00
1989	Loon	5.00
1990	Loon	5.00
1991	Loon	10.00
1992	Loon	6.00
1993	Loon	3.00
1994	Loon	4.00
1995	Loon	4.00
1996	Loon	12.00

BRILLIANT UNCIRCULATED SETS

NICKEL 7-COIN SETS

Date	Description	Buying Price
1997	Loon/Polar Bear	5.00
1998W	Loon/Polar Bear	8.00
1998	Loon/Polar Bear	8.00
1999	Loon/Polar Bear	6.00
1999	Loon/Nunavut	6.00
2000	Loon/Polar Bear	6.00
2000W	Loon/Polar Bear	6.00
2000	Loon/Polar Bears	6.00

PLATED STEEL 7-COIN SETS

Date	Description	Buying Price
2001P	Loon/Polar Bear	8.00
1952-2002P	Loon/Polar Bear	8.00
1952-2002P	Special	8.00
2003P	Loon/Polar Bear	8.00
2003WP	Special	8.00
2004P	Loon/Polar Bear	8.00
2005P	Loon/Polar Bear	8.00
2006P	Loon/Polar Bear	8.00

"OH CANADA!", BUNDLE OF JOY, and TINY TREASURES SETS

"OH CANADA!" NICKEL 6-COIN SETS

Date	Description	Buying Price
1994	Loon	6.00
1995	Peacekeeping	4.00
1996	Loon	7.00

"OH CANADA!" NICKEL 7-COIN SETS

Date	Description	Buying Price
1997	Flying Loon/Polar Bear	15.00
1998	Loon/Polar Bear	8.00
1998W	Loon/Polar Bear	8.00
1999	Loon/Polar Bear	8.00
2000	Loon/Polar Bear	4.00
2000W	Loon/Polar Bear	7.00

"OH CANADA!" MULTI-PLY PLATED STEEL 7-COIN SETS

Date	Description	Buying Price
2001P	Loon/Polar Bear	4.00
2002P	Loon/Polar Bear	8.00
2003P	Loon/Polar Bear	8.00
2004P	Loon/Polar Bear	8.00
2005P	Loon/Polar Bear	8.00
2006P	Loom/Polar Bear	8.00

"BUNDLE OF JOY/TINY TREASURES" NICKEL 6-COIN SETS

Date	Description	Buying Price
1995	Loon	7.00
1996	Loon	7.00

"BUNDLE OF JOY/TINY TREASURES" NICKEL 7-COIN SETS

Date	Description	Buying Price
1997	Loon/Polar Bear	8.00
1998	Loon/Polar Bear	8.00
1998W	Loon/Polar Bear	12.00
1999	Loon/Polar Bear	8.00
2000	Loon/Polar Bear	8.00
2000W	Loon/Polar Bear	8.00
2001	Loon/Polar Bears	4.00

"GIFT SETS" MULTI-PLY PLATED STEEL 7-COIN SETS

Date	Description	Buying Price
2001P	Loon/Polar Bear	4.00
2002P	Loon/Polar Bear	8.00
2003P	Loon/Polar Bear	8.00
2004P	Loon/Polar Bear	8.00
2005P	Loon/Polar Bear	8.00
2006P	Loon/Polar Bear	8.00

SPECIAL EDITION BRILLIANT UNCIRCULATED SETS

7-COIN SETS

Date	Description	Buying Price	Date	Description	Buying Price
2002P	Accession	10.00	2005P	Alberta Centenary	10.00
2003WP	Coronation	10.00	2005P	Saskatchewan Centenary	10.00

SPECIMEN SETS

SPECIMEN 7-COIN SETS

Date	Description	Buying Price
1971	Voyageur	2.00
1972	Voyageur	2.00
1973	Voyageur/RCMP, Small Bust	2.00
1974	Voyageur/RCMP, Large Bust	2.00
1975	Voyageur	2.00
1976	Voyageur	2.00
1977	Voyageur	2.00
1978	Voyageur	2.00
1979	Voyageur	2.00
1980	Voyageur	2.00

6-COIN SETS

Date	Description	Buying Price
1981	Voyageur	3.00
1982	Voyageur	3.00
1983	Voyageur	3.50
1984	Voyageur	3.50
1985	Voyageur	4.00
1986	Voyageur	4.00
1987	Voyageur	4.00
1988	Loon	7.00
1989	Loon	8.00

SPECIMEN 6-COIN SETS (cont.)

Date	Description	Buying Price
1990	Loon	8.00
1991	Loon	20.00
1992	Loon	12.00
1993	Loon	9.00
1994	Loon	10.00
1995	Loon	9.00
1996	Loon	12.00

SPECIMEN 7-COIN SETS

Date	Description	Buying Price
1997	Flying Loon	20.00
1998	Loon/Polar Bear	10.00
1999	Loon/Polar Bear	10.00
2000	Loon/Polar Bear	10.00
2000	Loon/Polar Bears	15.00
2001P	Loon/Polar Bear	5.00
2002P	Loon Family /Polar Bear	15.00
2003P	Loon/Polar Bear	15.00
2004P	Canada Goose/Polar Bear	15.00
2005P	Puffin/Polar Bear	15.00
2006P	Snowy Owl	15.00

PROOF SETS

PROOF 7-COIN SETS

Date	Description	Buying Price
1971	British Columbia	8.00
1972	Voyageur	14.00
1973	R.C.M.P., Small Bust	8.00
1973	R.C.M.P., Large Bust	125.00
1974	Winnipeg	8.00
1975	Calgary	8.00
1976	Parliament	8.00
1977	Jubilee	8.00
1978	Commonwealth Games	8.00
1979	Griffon	8.00
1980	Polar Bear	13.00
1981	Trans Canada	9.00
1982	Regina	8.00
1983	University Games	8.00
1984	Toronto	10.00
1985	National Parks	10.00
1986	Vancouver	10.00
1987	Davis Straits	10.00
1988	Ironworks	12.00
1989	MacKenzie River	12.00
1990	Henry Kelsey	12.00

PROOF 7-COIN SETS

Date	Description	Buying Price
1991	Frontenac	25.00
1992	Stagecoach	16.00
1993	Hockey	16.00
1994	RCMP	15.00
1994	RCMP Red Box	15.00
1995	Hudson's Bay	15.00
1995	Hudson's Bay Red Box	15.00
1996	John McIntosh	20.00

PROOF 8-COIN SETS

Date	Description	Buying Price
1997	Canada/Russia Hockey	20.00
1998	RCMP 125th Anniversary	25.00
1999	Juan Perez	40.00
2000	Discovery	35.00
2001	Ballet	25.00
2002	Jubilee	35.00
2003	Cobalt	35.00
2004	Ste Croix	35.00
2005	Canadian Flag	35.00
2006	Victoria Cross	35.00

MAPLE LEAF BULLION COINS

The Maple Leaf gold coins were first produced in 1979, the fractional or small sizes three years later in 1982, and the half-ounce size in 1986. In 1988 the four sizes; $5.00, $10.00, $20.00 and $50.00, of platinum were added. Expanding the range in 1993, $1.00 gold and platinum coins were issued, and again in 1994 $2.00 coins were placed on the market.

The price of Maple Leaf bullion coins is based on the spot market price in Canadian dollars on the day of purchase, times their gold content, less a small handling charge.

$50 $20 $10 $5

COIN SPECIFICATIONS

Denomination	Description	Content	Weight Tr. Oz.
$1	1/20 Maple	Gold or platinum	.050
$2	1/15 Maple	Gold or platinum	.667
$5	1/10 Maple	Gold or platinum	.100
$10	1/4 Maple	Gold or platinum	.250
$20	1/2 Maple	Gold or platinum	.500
$50	Maple	Gold or platinum	1.00
$5	Maple	Silver	1.00
$50	10 Maple	Silver	10.00

MAPLE LEAF PROOF BULLION ISSUES OF 1989

To commemorate the tenth anniversary of the Maple Leaf bullion program, the Royal Canadian Mint, in 1989, issued a series of proof condition silver, gold and platinum coins, individually and in sets. The single coins and sets were packaged in solid maple presentation cases with brown velvet liners.

Type	Description	Buying Price
Sets	Gold 4 coins: 1, 1/2, 1/4, 1/10 ounce maple	1,000.00
	Platinum 4 coins: 1, 1/2, 1/4, 1/10 ounce maple	1,950.00
	Gold and Platinum 1/10 ounce maple each, Silver 1 ounce Maple, 3 coins	175.00
	Gold, Platinum and Silver 3 coins: 1 ounce maple each	1,650.00
Singles	Gold, One Maple	650.00
	Silver, One Maple	20.00

PAPER MONEY OF CANADA

PROVINCE OF CANADA

1866 ISSUES

Denom.	Issue Date	Buying Price	Denom.	Issue Date	Buying Price
$1	1866	700.00	$10	1866	5,000.00
$2	1866	1,500.00	$20	1866	5,000.00
$5	1866	3,250.00	$50	1866	10,000.00

CANADA

1870 ISSUES

Plain	Series Letter A	Series Letter B

Denom.	Issue Date	Buying Price	Denom.	Issue Date	Buying Price
25-cent Plain	1870	15.00	25-cent Series B	1870	20.00
25-cent Series A	1870	100.00			

Note: The buying prices listed are for notes in **Very Good (VG)** condition.

1870 ISSUES

 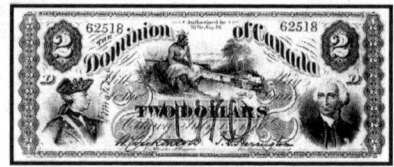

Denom.	Issue Date	Variety/Signature	Buying Price
$1	1870	Payable at Montreal or Toronto	400.00
$1	1870	Payable at Halifax	1,250.00
$1	1870	Payable at St. John	1,250.00
$2	1870	Payable at Montreal or Toronto	1,650.00
$2	1870	Payable at Halifax or St. John	2,750.00

1878 ISSUES

Denom.	Issue Date	Variety/Signature	Buying Price
$1	1878	Scalloped Frame, Payable at Montreal or Toronto	300.00
$1	1878	Scalloped Frame, Payable at St. John or Halifax	1,000.00
$1	1878	Lettered Frame, Payable at Montreal or Toronto	100.00
$1	1878	Lettered Frame, Payable at St. John or Halifax	1,000.00
$2	1878	Payable at Montreal or Toronto	1,000.00
$2	1878	Payable at St. John or Halifax	1,750.00

1882 AND 1887 ISSUES

Denom.	Issue Date	Variety/Signature	Buying Price
$4	1882		800.00
$2	1887	Plain,	350.00
$2	1887	Series A	1,000.00

Note: The buying prices listed are for notes in **Very Good (VG)** condition.

1897 AND 1898 ISSUES

  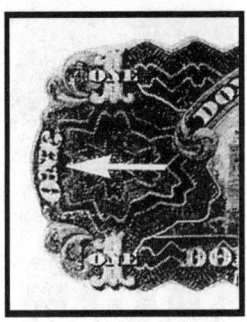

No "One" 1897   Inward "One" 1898   Outward "One" 1898

Denom.	Issue Date	Variety/Signature	Buying Price
$1	1897	Green face tint	225.00
$2	1897	Red-brown back	750.00
$2	1897	Dark brown back	125.00
$1	1898	Inward "One"	75.00
$1	1898	Outward "One"	50.00

1900 AND 1902 ISSUES

 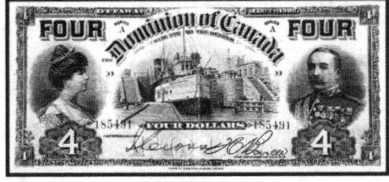

"4" on Top   "Four" on Top

Denom.	Issue Date	Variety/Signature	Buying Price
25-cent	1900	Courtney	3.00
25-cent	1900	Bouville	3.00
25-cent	1900	Saunders	3.00
$4	1900		400.00
$4	1902	"4" on Top	500.00
$4	1902	"Four" on Top	300.00

Note: The buying prices listed are for notes in **Very Good (VG)** condition.

1911 AND 1912 ISSUES

No Seal Seal over Five Seal Only

Denom.	Issue Date	Variety/Signature	Buying Price
$1	1911	Green Line or Black Line	35.00
$500	1911		10,000.00
$1,000	1911		8,000.00
$5	1912	No Seal	300.00
$5	1912	Seal over Five	325.00
$5	1912	Seal Only	300.00

1914 AND 1917 ISSUES

Denom.	Issue Date	Variety/Signature	Buying Price
$2	1914	No Seal	50.00
$2	1914	Seal over Two	125.00
$2	1914	Seal Only	75.00
$1	1917	No Seal	30.00
$1	1917	Seal over One	35.00
$1	1917	Black Seal	35.00

Note: The buying prices listed are for notes in **Very Good (VG)** condition.

1923 ISSUES

Denom.	Issue Date	Variety/Signature	Buying Price
25-cent	1923	Hyndman/Saunders	2.00
25-cent	1923	McCavour/Saunders	2.00
25-cent	1923	Campbell/Clark	2.00
$1	1923	Various Colour Seals	15.00
$1	1923	Purple Seal	50.00
$2	1923	Various Colour Seals	25.00
$2	1923	Green Seal	28.00
$2	1923	Bronze Seal	25.00

1924 AND 1925 ISSUES

Denom.	Issue Date	Variety/Signature	Buying Price
$5	1924	Queen Mary	1,750.00
$500	1925	George V	6,500.00
$1,000	1925	Queen Mary	7,000.00

Note: The buying prices listed are for notes in **Very Good (VG)** condition.

BANK OF CANADA

1935 ISSUES

Denom.	Variety	Buying Price	Denom.	Variety	Buying Price
$1	English text	12.00	$20	French text	250.00
$1	French text	20.00	$25	English text	850.00
$2	English text	22.00	$25	French text	1,000.00
$2	French text	40.00	$50	English text	500.00
$5	English text	40.00	$50	French text	700.00
$5	French text	50.00	$100	English text	250.00
$10	English text	40.00	$100	French text	500.00
$10	French text	60.00	$500	English or French	7,500.00
$20	English text	200.00	$1,000	English or French	1,400.00

Note: The buying prices listed are for notes in **Very Good (VG)** condition.

1937 ISSUES

IMPORTANT

Bank notes with tears, missing corners, pinholes or folding creases are not considered to be very fine (VF). Notes in poor condition are not collectable.

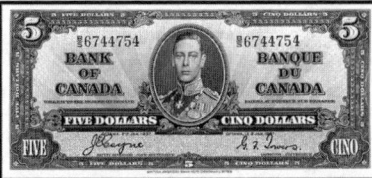

Denom.	Very Fine Buying Prices By Signature		
	Osborne	Gordon	Coyne
$1	10.00	4.00	4.00
$2	15.00	10.00	10.00
$5	50.00	9.00	9.00
$10	25.00	11.00	11.00
$20	30.00	21.00	21.00
$50	200.00	55.00	55.00
$100	125.00	100.00	100.00
$1,000	1,100.00	NI	NI

Note: 1. NI - Not issued.
   2. The buying prices listed are for notes in **Very Fine (VF)** condition.

1954 ISSUES

"DEVIL'S FACE" PORTRAIT

IMPORTANT

The buying prices listed below are for notes in very fine condition. The note must be clean, crisp, with no tears, creases, folds or marks of any kind or description folds.

THE DEVIL'S FACE NOTES

On the earliest notes of the 1954 issue, highlighted areas of the Queen's hair produced the illusion of a leering demonic face behind her ear. This was not the result of an error, nor was it, as some have asserted, the prank of an IRA sympathizer at the bank note company. It was merely the faithful reproduction of the original photograph. The portrait of the Queen with the devil's face outlined in her hair generated almost instant controversy.

ASTERISK NOTES

Asterisk notes are replacement notes, the first being spoiled in printing, cutting, etc., and replaced by an asterisk note. The asterisk is a small star-like symbol which appears before the prefix letters and serial number.

Denom.	Very Fine Buying Price by Signature			
	Coyne/Towers		Beattie/Coyne	
	Regular	Asterisk	Regular	Asterisk
$1	8.00	250.00	5.00	200.00
$2	10.00	350.00	8.00	300.00
$5	20.00	1,500.00	15.00	800.00
$10	15.00	500.00	10.00	300.00
$20	25.00	700.00	20.00	400.00
$50	50.00	NI	55.00	NI
$100	100.00	NI	110.00	NI
$1,000	1,100.00	NI	NI	NI

Note: 1. NI - Not Issued
2. The buying prices listed are for notes in **Very Fine (VF)** condition.

MODIFIED PORTRAIT

IMPORTANT

The buying prices listed below are for notes in uncirculated condition (new). The note must be clean, crisp, with no tears, creases, folds or marks of any kind or description.

MODIFIED PORTRAIT

The portrait was modified by darkening the highlights in the hair and thus removing the shading which had resulted in the devil's face. The modification of the face plates was made for most denominations in 1956, except for the $1,000 denomination, which was modified several years later.

Denom.	Uncirculated Buying Price by Signature							
	Beattie/Coyne		Beattie/Rasminsky		Bouey/Raminsky		Lawson/Bouey	
	Regular	Asterisk	Regular	Asterisk	Regular	Asterisk	Regular	Asterisk
$1	4.00	40.00	3.00	15.00	3.00	15.00	3.00	20.00
$2	12.00	100.00	4.00	8.00	5.00	15.00	5.00	18.00
$5	18.00	100.00	10.00	40.00	10.00	30.00	NI	NI
$10	20.00	150.00	12.50	30.00	NI	NI	NI	NI
$20	30.00	200.00	25.00	175.00	NI	NI	NI	NI
$50	100.00	NI	75.00	NI	NI	NI	100.00	NI
$100	150.00	NI	125.00	NI	NI	NI	150.00	NI
$1,000	1,400.00	NI	1,200.00	NI	1,200.00	NI	1,100.00	NI

Note: 1. NI - Not Issued
2. The above buying prices are for strictly uncirculated bank notes.

$1 CENTENNIAL 1967

For the centennial of Canada's Confederation a special $1 note was issued. The note has a single design and two types of serial numbers, regular serial numbers and a special number "1867 - 1967." The special series was available from the Bank of Canada as a collector's item, but examples were soon found in circulation. In addition, there was an asterisk note series for replacement notes.

Denom.	Issue Date	Variety	Uncirculated Buying Price
$1	1967	Commemorative Serial Number 1867-1967	1.05
$1	1967	Regular Serial Number	1.25
$1	1967	Asterisk Serial Number	8.00

1969 - 1975 ISSUE

This new series combined fine line engraving with subtle variations to make notes that are extremely difficult to counterfeit. The series features a new portrait of the Queen, as well as portraits of previous prime ministers of Canada.

IMPORTANT

The buying prices listed on the following page are for notes in uncirculated condition (new). The note must be clean, crisp, with no tears, creases, folds or marks of any kind or description.

1969-1975 ISSUES

ASTERISK AND "X" REPLACEMENT NOTES

Replacement of defective notes by asterisk notes was continued when the 1969-1975 issue was introduced. The highest denomination of the 1954 issue to be printed with asterisks was the $20; however, all denominations in the 1969-1975 issue, including the $50 and $100 notes, occur with asterisks in front of the two-letter prefix type.

When the triple-letter prefix notes were introduced in 1981, the use of the asterisk was discontinued. For triple-letter prefix notes, a replacement note was then designated by the use of an "X" for the third letter.

Asterisk Notes
BC-46aA

"X" Replacement Notes
BC-46A-i

			Uncirculated Buying Price by Signature					
	Beattie/Rasminsky		Bouey/Rasminsky		Lawson/Bouey		Crow/Bouey	
Denom.	Regular	Asterisk	Regular	Asterisk	Regular	X	Regular	X
$1	NI	NI	NI	NI	1.25	5.00	1.00	5.00
$2	NI	NI	NI	NI	4.00	12.00	4.00	125.00
$5	NI	NI	12.00	30.00	10.00	30.00	NI	NI
$10	25.00	50.00	20.00	50.00	15.00	30.00	15.00	40.00
$20	40.00	75.00	NI	NI	30.00	80.00	NI	NI
$50	NI	NI	NI	NI	90.00	300.00	60.00	100.00
$100	NI	NI	NI	NI	130.00	500.00	110.00	150.00

Note: 1. Lawson/Bouey signatures will be found with asterisks and 'X' for replacement notes.
2. NI - Not Issued

1979 ISSUES

The series beginning in 1979 is a modification of the previous issue. The face designs are similar, as is the colouration. The serial numbers are moved to the back of the note at the bottom, where the name of the Bank of Canada previously appeared. The black serial numbers are machine readable.

IMPORTANT

The buying prices listed below are for notes in uncirculated condition (new). The note must be clean, crisp, with no tears, creases, folds or marks of any kind or description.

REPLACEMENT NOTES

There are no asterisk notes in this issue. The replacement notes are designated by the second digit in the serial number.
The digit 1 following the first digit 3 of the $5 notes designates a replacement note. In the $20 denomination the replacement notes can be distinguished by "510" for the CBN company and "516" for the BABN company.

$5 Replacement Note $20 Replacement Note

Denom.	Uncirculated Buying Price by Signature					
	Lawson/Bouey		Crow/Bouey		Thiessen/Crow	
	Regular	Replace.	Regular	Replace.	Regular	Replace.
$5	10.00	150.00	20.00	300.00	NI	NI
$20	25.00	400.00	25.00	80.00	20.00	40.00

Note: Prices listed are buying prices for notes in new (uncirculated) condition.

1986 BIRD ISSUES

On March 14, 1986, the Bank of Canada introduced a new series of bank notes. The new designs were launched that year with the issue of the $2 and $5 notes. The $1 and $2 bank notes have since been replaced with $1 and $2 coins.

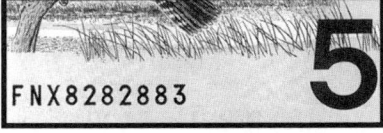

$5 Replacement Note

Denom.	Signature	Regular	Replacement
$2	Crow / Bouey	4.00	25.00
$5	Crow / Bouey	12.00	85.00

	Uncirculated Buying Price by Signature							
	Theissen/Crow		Bonin/Theissen		Knight/Thiessen		Knight/Dodge	
Denom.	Regular	Replace.	Regular	Replace.	Regular	Replace.	Regular	Replace.
$2	3.00	5.00	2.00	3.00	NI	NI	NI	NI
$5	5.00	10.00	5.00	35.00	5.00	20.00	5.00	10.00
$10	11.00	20.00	10.00	25.00	10.00	NI	NI	NI
$20	21.00	25.00	20.00	35.00	20.00	25.00	20.00	22.00
$50	55.00	60.00	50.00	NI	50.00	NI	50.00	55.00
$100	100.00	200.00	100.00	NI	100.00	NI	100.00	110.00
$1000	1,000.00	1,200.00	1,000.00	NI	1,000.00	NI	NI	NI

Note: Prices listed are buying prices for notes in new (uncirculated) condition

2001 JOURNEY ISSUES

Denom.	Uncirculated Buying Price by Signature		
	Knight/Thiessen	Knight/Dodge	Jenkins/Dodge
$5	NI	5.00	5.00
$10	10.00	10.00	10.00
$20	NI	NI	20.00
$50	NI	NI	50.00
$100	NI	NI	100.00

Note: 1. Prices listed are buying prices for notes in new (uncirculated) condition.
  2. No identifiable replacement notes have been printed for this issue.

NEWFOUNDLAND
PUBLIC WORKS CASH NOTES

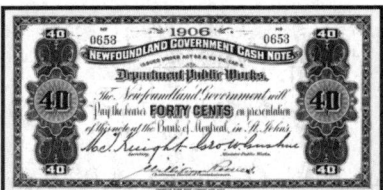

1901-1909

Denom.	Buying Price
40 cents	75.00
50 cents	85.00
80 cents	100.00
$1	125.00
$5	500.00

1910-1911

Denom.	Buying Price
25 cents	35.00
50 cents	35.00
$1	50.00
$2	450.00
$5	600.00

GOVERNMENT NOTES

Denom.	Buying Price
$1	40.00
$2	75.00

PRINCE EDWARD ISLAND

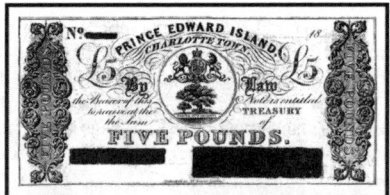

Denom.	Buying Price
1848-1870 5s	400.00
1848-1870 10s	400.00
1848-1870 £1	400.00
1848-1870 £2	400.00
1848-1870 £5	400.00
1872 $10	1,000.00
1872 $20	1,000.00

NOVA SCOTIA

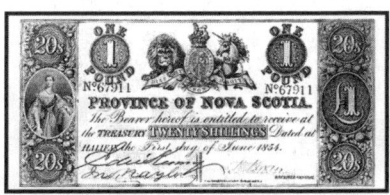

Denom.	Buying Price
1848-1854 £1	700.00
1861 $5	200.00

CANADIAN COLONIAL TOKENS

Canada has produced a great number of tokens of various kinds over the years. Tokens were used as a form of currency prior to the institution of the decimal currency system in 1858 (Colonial issues are not all tokens, some being regal coins). After Confederation, other kinds of tokens appeared, such as those for services, transportation and advertising purposes.

The prices in this section are for tokens in VG (very good) or F (fine) condition. Higher prices will be paid for rare issues or for tokens in VF (very fine) or better condition.

NEWFOUNDLAND TOKENS

Date and Description	Buying Price	Date and Description	Buying Price
Rutherford - St. John's	4.00	1858 Sailing Ship	175.00
Rutherford - Harbour Grace	4.00	1860 Fishery Rights	22.00
McAuslane	2,250.00		

PRINCE EDWARD ISLAND TOKENS

Date and Description	Buying Price	Date and Description	Buying Price
Holey Dollar Ring*	1,750.00	McCarthy Penny	1,750.00
Holey Dollar Plug*	1,750.00	Sheaf of Wheat	400.00
McCausland Penny	1,300.00	Speed The Plough	3.00

Note: * Forgeries exist and are worth considerably less.

PRINCE EDWARD ISLAND TOKENS

Date and Description	Buying Price	Date and Description	Buying Price
Fisheries & Agriculture	3.00	Fisheries & Agriculture	3.00
Self Government 1855 Prince Edward's	3.00	Ships Colonies 1815 One Penny	10.00
Self Government 1855 Prince Edward	3.00	Ships Colonies 1815 Publick Accommodation	10.00
Self Government 1857	3.00	Ships Colonies	3.50

Note: Tokens must be **VG (very good)** or better condition, with no discolouration or damage.

NOVA SCOTIA
SEMI-REGAL TOKENS

Date and Description	Buying Price
1823 Halfpenny	1.75
1823 Penny	3.00
1824 Halfpenny	1.75
1824 Penny	3.00
1832 Halfpenny	1.75
1832 Penny	3.00

Date and Description	Buying Price
1840 Halfpenny	1.75
1840 Penny	3.00
1843 Halfpenny	3.00
1843 Penny	6.00
1856 Halfpenny	3.00
1856 Penny	3.00

NOVA SCOTIA TOKENS

Date and Description	Buying Price	Date and Description	Buying Price
Broke - Halifax	4.00	Hosterman & Etter 1815	7.00
Convenience of Trade	13.00	Starr & Shannon	3.00
Carritt & Alport	6.00	Commercial Change	4.00
Hosterman & Etter	6.00	Miles W. White	4.00

NOVA SCOTIA TOKENS

Date and Description	Buying Price	Date and Description	Buying Price
John Alexr Barry	4.00	Trade & Navigation 1812	4.00
Halifax Nova Scotia	10.00	Trade & Navigation 1813	4.00
W. A. & S. Black's	10.00	Pure Copper Preferable	3.00
J. Brown	4.00	Success to Navigation	3.00
W. L. White's	18.50	N.S & N.B. Success	18.50

NEW BRUNSWICK TOKENS

Date and Description	Buying Price
1843 Halfpenny	1.25
1843 Penny	2.50
1854 Halfpenny	1.25
1854 Penny	2.50

Date and Description	Buying Price
McDermott	500.00
St. John	6.00
St. John's	4,000.00

LOWER CANADA TOKENS

Date and Description	Buying Price	Date and Description	Buying Price
Magdalen Island	25.00	Pro Bono Publico	2,250.00
Bank Token	3.00	Bank Token Halfpenny	1.75
Banque du Peuple, Maple Leaf	4.00	Bank Token Penny	3.00
Banque du Peuple, Wreath	1.75	Bank of Montreal, Sideview Halfpenny	375.00
		Bank of Montreal, Sideview Penny	575.00

LOWER CANADA TOKENS

Date and Description	Buying Price	Date and Description	Buying Price
Montreal Half Penny	3.00	Francis Mullins & Son	5.00
Canada Half Penny	3.00	R.W. Owen	5,000.00
For Public Accommodation	4.00	J. Shaw & Co.	4.00
T.S. Brown & Co.	3.00	J. Roy	22.50
Ths & Wm Molson	235.00	Agriculture & Commerce	1.75

LOWER CANADA TOKENS

Date and Description	Buying Price
Halfpenny Token 1812, Small Wreath	3.00
Halfpenny Token 1812, Large Wreath	3.00
Penny Token 1812	4.00
Victoria Nobis Est	4.00
R H Half Penny	4.00

Date and Description	Buying Price
To Facilitate Trade	
Military Bust 1825	4.00
Civilian Bust 1825	800.00
Spread Eagle	3.00
Halfpenny Token	5.00

LOWER CANADA TOKENS

Date and Description	Buying Price	Date and Description	Buying Price
Seated Justice	3.00	Commercial Change	3.00
Bust/Ships Colonies	4.00	Bust and Harp	6.00

WELLINGTON TOKENS

Date and Description	Buying Price	Date and Description	Buying Price
Field Marshal Wellington	3.00	The Illustrious Wellington	3.00
Marquis Wellington	4.00	Battle Token	3.00

UPPER CANADA TOKENS

Date and Description	Buying Price
Copper Company	235.00
Lesslie Halfpenny	5.00
Lesslie Twopenny	75.00
No Labour No Bread	3.00
Sir Isaac Brock	3.00

Date and Description	Buying Price
Success To Commerce	3.00
Upper & Lower Canada	22.50
Commercial Change 1815	22.50
Commerical Change 1820	3.00

UPPER CANADA TOKENS

Date and Description	Buying Price	Date and Description	Buying Price
Commercial Change 1821		To Facilitate Trade	
Cask Marked Upper Canada	22.50	1823	3.00
Cask Marked Jamaica	285.00	1833	1.75
Province of Upper Canada	12.00	Commercial Change 1833	3.00

PROVINCE OF CANADA TOKENS

PROVINCE OF CANADA TOKENS

Date and Description	Buying Price	Date and Description	Buying Price
Bank of Montreal		Quebec Bank, 1852 Halfpenny	1.75
1842, 1844 Halfpenny	1.75	Penny	3.00
1845 Halfpenny	1,500.00	Bank of Upper Canada 1850-1857	
1837 Penny	60.00	Halfpenny	1.75
1842 Penny	4.00	Penny	3.00

ANONYMOUS AND MISCELLANEOUS TOKENS

Date and Description	Buying Price	Date and Description	Buying Price
For General Accommodation	3.00	Pure Copper Preferable	3.00
Success to Trade	15.00	North American	18.50

BRITISH COLUMBIA TOKENS

Date and Description	Buying Price
1862 Pattern Gold $10	50,000.00
1862 Pattern Gold $20	50,000.00

NORTH WEST COMPANY

Date and Description	Buying Price
1820 North West Company Token	600.00

HUDSON'S BAY COMPANY

Date and Description	Buying Price
Hudson's Bay Company Tokens Set of four (1, ½, ¼, 1/8)	55.00

TRANSPORTATION TOKENS

Date and Description	Buying Price
Bridge Tokens, each	100.00
Montreal & Lachine Railroad	50.00

CANADIAN MEDALS

WAR MEDALS 1812 TO 1885

Army Gold Cross

Naval General Service Medal

Army Gold Medal

Canadian General Service Medal

Army General Service Medal

Egyptian Medal

Date and Description	Buying Price
Army Gold Cross	15,000.00
Army Gold Medal	5,500.00
Army General Service Medal 1812-1814	
Fort Detroit Bar	1,750.00
Chateauguay Bar	1,750.00
Chrysler's Farm Bar	1,750.00
Naval General Service Medal 1812-1814	175.00

Date and Description	Buying Price
Canadian General Service Medal	
Fenian Raid Bar 1866	125.00
Fenian Raid Bar 1870	125.00
Red River Bar 1870	500.00
Egyptian Medal*	
The Nile Bar	500.00
Kirbekan Bar	500.00
*Awarded to Canadian Boatmen	

WAR MEDALS 1885 TO 1914

Khedive's Bronze Star

1914 Star

North West Canada Medal

1914-1915 Star

South Africa Medal

British War Medal

Date and Description	Buying Price
Khedive's Bronze Star	20.00
North West Canada Medal 1885	175.00
Saskatchewan Bar	225.00
Queen's South Africa	
1899-1900 on reverse	2,250.00
Dates removed	25.00
King's South Africa	25.00

Date and Description	Buying Price
1914 Star*	850.00
1914-1915 Star	5.00
British War Medal	10.00
Groups**	
Star, British War Medal (2)	25.00
Star, Allied Victory Medal British War Medal (3)	30.00

*Canadian Star awarded only to 2nd. Field Hospital.
**Groups to Canadian Veterans, named to same person

WAR MEDALS 1914 TO 1945

Allied Victory Medal

Canadian Defence Medal

Merchantile Marine War Medal

Canadian WW II 1939-1945 War Medal

Canadian Volunteer Service Medal

Atlantic
Air Crew Europe
Africa
France and Germany
Italy
Pacific
Burma

Date and Description	Buying Price
Allied Victory Medal	5.00
Merchantile Marine War Medal	10.00
Canadian Volunteer Service Medal	10.00
Defence Medal	10.00
1939-1945 War Medal	10.00

Date and Description	Buying Price
1939-1945 Star	5.00
Atlantic Star	15.00
Air Crew Europe	50.00
Africa Star	5.00
France and Germany Star	5.00
Italy Star	5.00
Pacific Star	10.00
Burma Star	10.00

Note: The Canadian Volunteer Service Medal, the Canadian Defence Medal and the World War II Medal are issued in silver. Britain and other Commonwealth countries issued cupro-nickel medals.

WAR MEDALS
1951 TO 1973

COMMEMORATIVE MEDALS

Canadian Korean Medal

1911 Coronation Medal

United Nations Korea Medal

1935 Silver Jubilee Medal

United Nations Emergency Medal

1937 Coronation Medal

Date and Description	Buying Price
Canadian Korean War Medal, English	25.00
Canadian Korean War Medal, French	35.00
United Nations Korea Medal	15.00
United Nations Emergency Medal	15.00
United Nations Medal 1960 to present	15.00
International Commission Medal 1967	15.00
International Commission Medal 1973	15.00

Date and Description	Buying Price
King George V	
Coronation Medal - 1911	20.00
Silver Jubilee Medal - 1935	15.00
King George VI	
Coronation Medal - 1937	15.00

COMMEMORATIVE MEDALS

MEDALS FOR VALOUR AND SERVICE

1953 Coronation Medal

Victoria Cross

1977 Silver Jubilee Medal

Distinguished Service Order

1967 Canadian Centennial Medal

Order of St. Michael and St. George

Date and Description	Buying Price
Queen Elizabeth II	
Coronation Medal - 1953	15.00
Silver Jubilee Medal - 1977	35.00
Canadian Centennial Medal - 1967	25.00

Date and Description	Buying Price
Victoria Cross	35,000.00
Awarded to a Canadian	60,000.00
Distinguished Service Order	200.00
Order of St. Michael and St. George	200.00

MEDALS FOR VALOUR AND SERVICE

Distinguished Service Cross

Air Force Medal

Distinguished Flying Cross

Military Medal

Air Force Cross

British Empire Medal

Date and Description	Buying Price
Distinguished Service Cross	250.00
Distinguished Flying Cross	350.00
Air Force Cross	400.00

Date and Description	Buying Price
Air Force Medal	125.00
Military Medal	175.00
British Empire Medal	50.00

COINS OF THE UNITED STATES

MINT MARKS

The United States decimal coinage is identified by the following mint marks:
- C — Charlotte, North Carolina
- CC — Carson City, Nevada
- D — Dahlonega, Georgia (gold coins only)
- D — Denver, Colorado (1906 to date)
- O — New Orleans, Louisiana
- S — San Francisco, California
- P — Philadelphia, Pennsylvania

HALF CENTS

Liberty Cap

Date and Mint Mark	Buying Price
1793 Head Facing Left	800.00
1794	150.00
1795	100.00
1796	3,500.00
1797	150.00

Draped Bust

Date and Mint Mark	Buying Price
1800	20.00
1802	350.00
1803-1808	20.00

Classic Head

Date and Mint Mark	Buying Price
1809-1810	20.00
1811	75.00
1825 to 1835	18.00

Coronet Head

Date and Mint Mark	Buying Price
1849 to 1857	10.00

IMPORTANT NOTICE:
Buying prices are for coins in VG condition.

LARGE CENTS

Flowing Hair

Date and Mint Mark	Buying Price
1793 Chain Reverse	1,500.00
1793 Wreath Reverse	750.00

Liberty Cap

Date and Mint Mark	Buying Price
1793	1,200.00
1794	75.00
1795	50.00
1796	75.00

Draped Bust

Date and Mint Mark	Buying Price
1796	65.00
1797	45.00
1798	25.00
1799	800.00
1800 to 1803	25.00
1804	250.00
1805 to 1807	20.00

Classic Head

Date and Mint Mark	Buying Price
1808	20.00
1809	40.00
1810	15.00
1811	30.00
1812 to 1814	20.00

Coronet Head

Date and Mint Mark	Buying Price
1816 to 1820	5.00
1821	20.00
1822	8.00
1823	25.00
1824 to 1838	5.00
1839 to 1856	5.00
1857	15.00

SMALL CENTS

Flying Eagle

Date and Mint Mark	Buying Price
1856	3,000.00
1857 to 1858	6.00

Indian Head

Date and Mint Mark	Buying Price
1859	4.00
1860 to 1865	3.00
1866 to 1868	12.00
1869 to 1872	20.00
1873 to 1876	7.00
1877	225.00
1878	9.00
1879 to 1886	.75
1887 to 1908	.25
1908S	20.00
1909	.75
1909S	110.00

Lincoln Head Wheat Ears

Date and Mint Mark	Buying Price
1909	.50
1909VDB	1.00
1909S	20.00
1909S VDB	175.00
1910 to 1914	.10
1914D	50.00
1915D to 1931D	.05
1931S	17.00
1932 to 1958	.01
1955 Double Die	100.00

Lincoln Head Memorial

Date and Mint Mark	Buying Price
1959 to 2006	.01

TWO CENTS

Date and Mint Mark	Buying Price
1864 to 1871	4.00
1872	75.00
1873 Proofs only	500.00

THREE CENTS

Silver

Date and Mint Mark	Buying Price
1851 to 1862	7.00
1863 to 1872	100.00
1873 Proofs only	150.00

Nickel

Date and Mint Mark	Buying Price
1865 to 1874	4.00
1875 to 1876	5.00
1877 to 1878 Proofs only	200.00
1879 to 1880	12.00
1881	4.00
1882	20.00
1883	40.00
1884 to 1887	100.00
1888	15.00
1889	20.00

FIVE CENTS NICKEL

Shield

Date and Mint Mark	Buying Price
1866 to 1870	5.00
1871	14.00
1872 to 1876	6.00
1877 and 1878 Proofs only	100.00
1879 to 1881	75.00
1882 to 1883	4.00

Liberty Head

Date and Mint Mark	Buying Price
1883 to 1884	4.00
1885	125.00
1886	65.00
1887 to 1896	1.00
1897 to 1912D	.25
1912S	35.00

Indian Head or Buffalo Type

Date and Mint Mark	Buying Price
1913 and 1913D	2.00
1913S	10.00
1914 to 1918	1.00
1918D 8/7	500.00
1919 to 1938	.15

Jefferson Type

Date and Mint Mark	Buying Price
1938 to 2003	.05

HALF DIMES

Flowing Hair

Date and Mint Mark	Buying Price
1794	300.00
1795	200.00

Draped Bust

Date and Mint Mark	Buying Price
1796 to 1797	250.00
1800 to 1801	200.00
1802	5,000.00
1803 to 1805	200.00

Capped Bust

Date and Mint Mark	Buying Price
1829 to 1837	9.00

Liberty Seated

Date and Mint Mark	Buying Price
1837 No Stars	10.00
1837O No Stars	20.00
1838 to 1845	3.00
1846	50.00
1847 to 1862	4.00
1863	40.00
1863S	8.00
1864	75.00
1864S	10.00
1865	65.00
1865S	7.00
1866	60.00
1866S	7.00
1867	100.00
1867S to 1873S	4.00

DIMES

Draped Bust

Date and Mint Mark	Buying Price
1796 to 1797	500.00
1798 to 1807	100.00

Capped Bust

Date and Mint Mark	Buying Price
1809 to 1811	30.00
1814 to 1821	7.00
1822	150.00
1823 to 1837	7.00

Liberty Seated

Date and Mint Mark	Buying Price
1837O and 1838O No stars	12.00
1838 to 1840O Stars	5.00
1841 to 1843	5.00
1843O	15.00
1844	75.00
1845 to 1845O	5.00
1846	25.00
1847 to 1856	4.00
1856S	40.00
1857 to 1860	4.00
1858S	30.00
1859S	35.00
1860O	125.00
1861 to 1862	4.00
1863	75.00
1863S	7.00
1864	5.00
1864S	6.00
1865	65.00
1865S	6.00
1866	85.00
1866S	7.00
1867	100.00
1867S	7.00
1868 to 1874	4.00
1871CC	600.00
1872CC	175.00
1873CC Arrows	400.00
1874CC Arrows	800.00
1875 to 1878	2.00
1878CC	17.00
1879 to 1881	35.00
1882 to 1885	2.00
1885S	125.00
1886 to 1891	2.00

Barber

Date and Mint Mark	Buying Price
1892 to 1895	2.00
1895O	100.00
1896O	30.00
1897 to 1916	.50

Mercury Head

Date and Mint Mark	Buying Price
1916	1.00
1916D	300.00
1917 to 1945	.50
1921	20.00
1921D	35.00

Roosevelt - Silver

Date and Mint Mark	Buying Price
1946 to 1964	.50

Roosevelt - Clad

Date and Mint Mark	Buying Price
1965 to 2006	.10

TWENTY CENTS

Date and Mint Mark	Buying Price
1875 to 1876	25.00
1877 to 1878 Proofs only	400.00

QUARTER DOLLAR

Draped Bust

Date and Mint Mark	Buying Price
1796	2,500.00
1804	700.00
1805 to 1807	70.00

Capped Bust

Date and Mint Mark	Buying Price
1815 to 1822	20.00
1823/2	4,000.00
1824 to 1828	15.00
1831 to 1838 Reduced Size	17.00

Liberty Seated

Date and Mint Mark	Buying Price
1838 to 1849	6.00
1849O	100.00
1850 to 1851	8.00
1851O	50.00
1852	10.00
1852O	60.00

Date and Mint Mark	Buying Price
1853 to 1865	6.00
1862S to 1865S	15.00
1864S	80.00
1866 to 1867S	50.00
1868 to 1870	20.00
1870CC and 1871CC	600.00
1871 to 1878CC	7.00
1871S	65.00
1872CC	150.00
1872S	200.00
1878S to 1888	25.00
1888S	5.00
1889 and 1890	20.00
1891O	30.00
1891 and 1891S	5.00

Washington - Silver

Date and Mint Mark	Buying Price
1932 to 1964	1.25
1927S	2.00
1932D	.25
1932S	.25

Washington - Clad

Date and Mint Mark	Buying Price
1965 to 1975	.25

200th Bi-Centennial

Date and Mint Mark	Buying Price
1976	.25

Barber

Date and Mint Mark	Buying Price
1892 to 1896	2.00
1896S	200.00
1897 to 1901	2.00
1901S	1,750.00
1902 to 1913	2.00
1913S	350.00
1914 to 1916D	2.00

Standing Liberty

Date and Mint Mark	Buying Price
1916	1,500.00
1917 to 1924	8.00
1923S	100.00
1925 to 1930	2.00

Note: Coins must be in very good condition or better to command these prices, coins grading good or less will command lower prices.

Washington - Clad

Date and Mint Mark	Buying Price
1977 to 1999	.25

State Quarters

Date and Mint Mark	Buying Price
1999 to 2006	.25

HALF DOLLARS
Flowing Hair

Date and Mint Mark	Buying Price
1794	900.00
1795	165.00

Draped Bust

Date and Mint Mark	Buying Price
1796 15 Stars	5,000.00
1796 16 Stars	5,000.00
1797 15 Stars	5,000.00
1801 to 1802	75.00
1803 to 1807	50.00

Capped Bust

Date and Mint Mark	Buying Price
1807	20.00
1808 to 1814	12.00
1815	325.00

Date and Mint Mark	Buying Price
1817 to 1836	12.00
1837 to 1839	12.00
1839O	45.00

Liberty Seated

Date and Mint Mark	Buying Price
1839 to 1852O	10.00
1850	50.00
1851	50.00
1852	75.00
1853O No Arrows	20,000.00
1853 to 1855	5.00
1855S Arrows	75.00
1856 to 1865S	6.00
1866 to 1873CC	5.00
1870CC	200.00
1871CC	50.00
1873 to 1874S	5.00
1875 to 1878	5.00
1878CC	50.00
1878S	3,000.00
1879 to 1890	60.00
1891	10.00

Barber

Date and Mint Mark	Buying Price
1892	6.00
1892O	75.00
1892S	60.00
1893 to 1897	3.00
1897O	30.00
1897S	30.00
1898 to 1915	3.00

Liberty Walking

Date and Mint Mark	Buying Price
1916 to 1920	2.50
1921	60.00
1921D	100.00
1923 to 1947	2.50

Franklin

Date and Mint Mark	Buying Price
1948 to 1963	2.50

Kennedy - Silver

Date and Mint Mark	Buying Price
1964	2.50

Kennedy - Silver Clad

Date and Mint Mark	Buying Price
1965 to 1970	1.30

Kennedy - Copper Clad

Date and Mint Mark	Buying Price
1971 to 2006	.50

SILVER DOLLARS

Flowing Hair

Date and Mint Mark	Buying Price
1794	12,000.00
1795	425.00

Draped Bust

Date and Mint Mark	Buying Price
1795	400.00
1796 to 1798	400.00
1798 to 1803	400.00

Note: Coins must grade very good (VG) or better to command prices listed.

Liberty Seated

Date and Mint Mark	Buying Price
1840 to 1873	50.00
1851 and 1852	1,200.00
1854	300.00
1855	200.00
1858 Proofs only	900.00
1870CC	125.00
1870S	20,000.00
1871CC	650.00
1872CC	300.00
1872S	75.00
1873CC	1,250.00

Liberty Head

Date and Mint Mark	Buying Price
1878 to 1892	10.00
1878CC to 1881CC	25.00
1882CC to 1884CC	20.00
1885CC	60.00
1889CC	300.00
1893CC	100.00
1890O to 1893O	10.00
1893S	1,000.00
1894	300.00
1895	5,000.00
1895O	65.00
1895S	50.00
1896 to 1903	10.00
1903O	50.00
1904 to 1921	10.00

Peace

Date and Mint Mark	Buying Price
1921	20.00
1922 to 1927	10.00
1928	100.00
1928S to 1935S	10.00

Eisenhower

Date and Mint Mark	Buying Price
1971 to 1978	1.00

Susan B. Anthony

Date and Mint Mark	Buying Price
1979 to 1981	1.00

TRADE DOLLARS

Date and Mint Mark	Buying Price
1873 to 1878	20.00
1878CC	100.00
1879 to 1883	300.00

GOLD DOLLARS

Type 1 Liberty Head

Date and Mint Mark	Buying Price
1849 to 1854	75.00

Type 2 Indian Head, Small

Date and Mint Mark	Buying Price
1854 to 1855	100.00
1855C	400.00
1855D	1,500.00
1855O	150.00
1856S	250.00

Type 3 Indian Head, Large

Date and Mint Mark	Buying Price
1856 to 1889	75.00
1856D	1,000.00
1860D	750.00
1861D	1,500.00
1875	600.00

GOLD 2 ½ DOLLARS

Capped Bust Right

Date and Mint Mark	Buying Price
1796	5,000.00
1797 to 1807	1,250.00

Capped Bust Left

Date and Mint Mark	Buying Price
1808	5,000.00

Capped Head Left

Date and Mint Mark	Buying Price
1821 to 1827	1,000.00
1829 to 1833	1,500.00
1834 No Motto	2,000.00

Classic Head

Date and Mint Mark	Buying Price
1834 to 1839	125.00

Coronet Head

Date and Mint Mark	Buying Price
1840 to 1907	90.00
1848 California	3,000.00
1854D	1,000.00
1854S	12,500.00
1855D	500.00
1856D	2,500.00
1875	1,000.00

Indian Head

Date and Mint Mark	Buying Price
1908 to 1929	100.00
1911D	500.00

3 DOLLARS

Date and Mint Mark	Buying Price
1854 to 1873	350.00
1854D	2,500.00
1873 Closed 3	1,000.00
1880 to 1889	300.00

4 DOLLARS

Date and Mint Mark	Buying Price
1879 to 1880	20,000.00

GOLD 5 DOLLARS

Capped Bust - Small Eagle

Date and Mint Mark	Buying Price
1795 to 1797	3,500.00
1798	10,000.00

Capped Bust - Heraldic Eagle

Date and Mint Mark	Buying Price
1795 to 1797	1,500.00
1798 to 1807	800.00

Capped Draped Bust Left

Date and Mint Mark	Buying Price
1807 to 1812	800.00

Capped Head

Date and Mint Mark	Buying Price
1813 to 1820	800.00
1815	10,000.00
1819	2,500.00
1821	2,500.00
1823	800.00
1824 to 1826	1,750.00
1829	5,000.00
1830 to 1834	4,000.00

Classic Head

Date and Mint Mark	Buying Price
1834 to 1838	120.00
1838C	400.00
1838D	350.00

Coronet Head

Date and Mint Mark	Buying Price
1839 to 1908	110.00
1842C	500.00
1854S	30,000.00
1861C	500.00
1861D	1,000.00
1864S	1,000.00
1865S	500.00
1870CC	1,000.00
1875	5,000.00
1878CC	750.00

Indian Head

Date and Mint Mark	Buying Price
1908 to 1916	125.00
1909O	500.00
1929	1,500.00

GOLD 10 DOLLARS

Capped Bust Right

Date and Mint Mark	Buying Price
Small Eagle, 1795 to 1797	5,000.00
Heraldic Eagle, 1797 to 1804	2,000.00

Coronet Head

Date and Mint Mark	Buying Price
1838 to 1907	300.00
1858	1,200.00
1859O	1,000.00
1859S	600.00
1863	1,000.00
1864S	1,200.00
1865S	1,000.00
1866S	600.00
1867S	500.00
1870CC	2,000.00
1871CC	600.00
1872	600.00
1872CC	800.00
1873	1,200.00
1873CC	1,500.00
1875	12,000.00
1875CC	1,000.00
1876	900.00
1876CC	900.00
1877	600.00
1877CC	700.00
1878CC	1,000.00
1879CC	1,700.00
1879O	500.00
1883O	800.00

$10 Indian Head

Date and Mint Mark	Buying Price
1907 to 1932	325.00
1920S	2,000.00
1930S	2,000.00
1933	20,000.00

GOLD $20 DOLLARS
Liberty

Date and Mint Mark	Buying Price
1850 to 1907	600.00
1854O	15,000.00
1855O	800.00
1856O	20,000.00
1859O	1,000.00
1860O	850.00
1861O	700.00
1866S	800.00
1870CC	25,000.00
1871CC	1,500.00
1872CC	600.00
1879O	1,500.00
1881	1,000.00
1882	2,000.00
1885	1,500.00
1886	2,500.00
1891	900.00
1891CC	1,000.00

$20 St. Gaudens

Date and Mint Mark	Buying Price
1907 MCMVII	2,000.00
1907 to 1916	600.00
1920S	3,000.00
1921	4,000.00
1922 to 1928	600.00
1927D	50,000.00
1927S	1,500.00
1929	2,000.00
1930 to 1932	2,500.00

GOLD COMMEMORATIVE COINS

Date and Mint Mark	Buying Price
1903 $1 Louisiana Purchase	150.00
1904-05 $1 Lewis & Clark Exposition	200.00
1915S $1 Panama-Pacific Exposition	150.00
1916 $1 McKinley Memorial	150.00
1917 $1 McKinley Memorial	175.00
1922 $1 Grant Memorial, With Star	450.00
1922 $1 Grant Memorial, Without Star	450.00
1915S $2.50 Panama-Pacific Exposition	550.00
1926 $2.50 Philadelphia Sesquicentennial	125.00
1984P and D $10 Olympic	300.00
1984S $10 Olympic	300.00
1984W $10 Olympic	300.00
1986W $5 Liberty	150.00
1987W $5 Constitution	150.00
1988W $5 Oylmpic	150.00
1989W $5 Congress	150.00
1991W $5 Mount Rushmore	150.00
1992W $5 Olympic	150.00
1992W $5 Columbus	150.00
1993W $5 Bill of Rights	150.00
1994W $5 World Cup	150.00
1995W $5 Civil War	250.00
1995W $5 Olympic Torch	200.00
1995W $5 Olympic Stadium	200.00
1995W $5 WWII	150.00
1996W $5 Flag Bearer	200.00
1996W $5 Cauldron	200.00
1996W $5 Smithsonian	300.00
1997W $5 F.D.R.	150.00
1997W $5 Jackie Robinson	800.00
1999W $5 George Washington	150.00
2000W $10 Library of Congress	400.00
2001W $5 Capitol Visitor Centre	200.00
2002W $5 Salt Lake City Olympics	150.00
2003W $5 First Flight	150.00

SILVER COMMEMORATIVE COINS

Date and Mint Mark	Buying Price
1982D or S 50¢ George Washington	2.00
1983P, D or S $1 Los Angeles Olympics	5.00
1984P, D or S, $1 Los Angeles Olympics	5.00
1986D or S 50¢ Statue of Liberty	2.00
1986P or S $1 Statue of Liberty	5.00
1987P or S $1 Constitution	5.00
1988D or S $1 Seoul Olympiad	5.00
1989D or S 50¢ Congress	2.00
1989D or S $1 Congress	8.00
1990W or P $1 Eisenhower	8.00
1991D $1 Korean War	6.00
1991D or S 50¢ Mount Rushmore	7.00
1991D or S $1 USO	6.00
1991P or S $1 Mount Rushmore	12.00
1992D or W $1 White House	10.00
1992D or S $1 XXV Olympiad	10.00
1992D or S 50¢ Christopher Columbus	4.00
1992D or P $1 Christopher Columbus	10.00
1992P or S 50¢ XXV Olympiad	3.00
1993D or W $1 D-Day	20.00
1993-1994P or S $1 Thomas Jefferson	10.00
1993W or S 50¢ Bill of Rights	5.00
1994D or P 50¢ World Cup	4.00
1994D or S $1 World Cup	15.00
1994D or S $1 U.S. Capitol	10.00
1994W or P $1 Vietnam Veterans Mem.	30.00
1994W or P $1 U.S. Prisoner of War Mem.	30.00
1994W or P $1 Women in Military	20.00
1995D $1 Olympics, Gymnastics	30.00
1995D $1 Olympics, Paralympic	30.00
1995D $1 Olympics, Track & Field	30.00
1995D $1 Olympics, Cycling	30.00
1995D or S $1 Bill of Rights	7.00
1995P 50¢ 50th Anniversary WWII	10.00
1995P or S $1 Civil War Battlefields	25.00
1995P $1 Cycling (PR)	15.00
1995P $1 Gymnastics (PR)	20.00
1995P $1 Paralympics (PR)	20.00
1995P $1 Track & Field (PR)	15.00
1995S 50¢ Civil War Battlefields	15.00
1995S 50¢ Olympics, Basketball	8.00
1995S 50¢ Olympics, Baseball	8.00
1995S 50¢ Olympics, Swimming	30.00
1995S 50¢ Olympics, Soccer	30.00
1995 W or P $1 Special Olympics	10.00
1996D $1 Olympics, Tennis	60.00
1996D $1 Olympics, Paralympic	100.00
1996D $1 Olympics, Rowing	100.00
1996D P $1 Olympics, Jump	100.00
1996D $1 Smithsonian (MS)	35.00
1996P $1 Smithsonian (PR)	15.00
1996P $1 High Jump	15.00
1996P $1 Paralympics (PR)	20.00
1996P $1 Rowing (PR)	20.00
1996P $1 Tennis (PR)	20.00
1996S $1 Community Service (MS)	75.00
1996S $1 Community Service (PR)	25.00
1997P $1 Botanic Gardens (MS & PR)	15.00
1997P $1 Law Enforcement (MS & PR)	50.00
1997S $1 Robinson (MS & PR)	20.00
1998S $1 Black Patriots (MS & PR)	50.00

WORLD GOLD COINS

This partial listing of common world gold coins indicates the prices dealers are willing to pay based on the Canadian dollar gold price as at August 1, 2006 ($650.00 U.S., 1.1250 Can./U.S.). Prices will fluctuate with the market price of gold, and the Canadian-U.S. dollar exchange rate.

AUSTRIA

Date and Denom.	Fine Gold Content Oz.	Buying Price
1912 10K	0.0980	53.00
1915 20K	0.1960	106.00
1915 100K	0.9803	530.00
1915 1D	0.1109	61.00
1914 4D	0.4438	225.00
1892 10Fr	0.0933	51.00
1892 20Fr*	0.1867	102.00

BAHAMAS

Date and Denom.	Fine Gold Content Oz.	Buying Price
1967 $10	0.1177	64.00
1971 $10	0.1177	64.00
1972 $10	0.0940	51.00
1967 $20	0.2355	128.00
1971 $20*	0.2355	128.00
1972 $20	0.1880	103.00
1967 $50	0.5888	320.00
1971 $50	0.5888	320.00
1972 $50	0.4708	258.00
1967 $100	1.1776	645.00
1971 $100	1.1776	645.00
1972 $100	0.9420	516.00

BELGIUM

Date and Denom.	Fine Gold Content Oz.	Buying Price
1867 to 1914 20Fr	0.1867	102.00

BERMUDA

Date and Denom.	Fine Gold Content Oz.	Buying Price
1970 $20	0.2355	130.00
1977 $50	0.1172	64.00
1975 $100*	0.2304	126.00
1977 $100	0.2344	128.00

CAYMAN ISLANDS

Date and Denom.	Fine Gold Content Oz.	Buying Price
1972 $25*	0.2532	138.00
1974 $50	0.1823	100.00
1974 $100	0.3646	200.00
1975 $100	0.3646	200.00
1977 $100	0.3646	200.00

* Coin illustrated

CHILE

Date and Denom.	Fine Gold Content Oz.	Buying Price
1898 to 1900 5p	0.0883	48.00
1896 to 1901 10p*	0.1766	96.00
1896 to 1917 20p	0.3532	200.00
1926 to 1980 100p	0.5886	325.00

COLUMBIA

Date and Denom.	Fine Gold Content Oz.	Buying Price
1913 to 1929 2 ½ p	0.1177	64.00
1913 to 1930 5p	0.2355	128.00
1919 and 1924 10p	0.4710	255.00
1973 1500p*	0.5527	303.00

FRANCE

Date and Denom.	Fine Gold Content Oz.	Buying Price
1856 to 1869 5Fr	0.0467	26.00
1854 to 1914 10Fr	0.0933	52.00
1809 to 1914 20Fr*	0.1867	102.00
1810 to 1838 40Fr	0.3734	205.00
1855 to 1864 50Fr	0.4667	255.00
1855 to 1913 100Fr	0.9335	510.00

* Coin illustrated

GERMANY

Date and Denom.	Fine Gold Content Oz.	Buying Price
1872 to 1914 10DM	0.1152	63.00
1871 to 1914 20DM*	0.2304	125.00

GREAT BRITAIN

Date and Denom.	Fine Gold Content Oz.	Buying Price
1863 to 1915 ½ Sov.	0.1177	64.00
1871 to 1968 Sov.*	0.2354	128.00
1887 Two Pound	0.4708	256.00
1897 Two Pound	0.4708	256.00
1902 Two Pound	0.4708	256.00
1911 Two Pound	0.4708	256.00
1937 Two Pound	0.4708	256.00
1887 Five Pound	1.1773	645.00
1897 Five Pound	1.1773	645.00
1902 Five Pound	1.1773	645.00
1911 Five Pound	1.1773	645.00
1937 Five Pound	1.1773	645.00

IRAN

Date and Denom.	Fine Gold Content Oz.	Buying Price
1971 500R	0.1883	103.00
1971 750R*	0.2827	155.00
1971 1000R	0.3770	206.00
1971 2000R	0.7541	413.00

ITALY

Date and Denom.	Fine Gold Content Oz.	Buying Price
1932 to 1860 10L	0.0931	51.00
1831 to 1860 20L*	0.1867	103.00
1822 to 1831 40L	0.3733	205.00
1832 to 1844 100L	0.9332	510.00

NETHERLANDS

Date and Denom.	Fine Gold Content Oz.	Buying Price
1900 to 1937 1D*	0.1109	61.00
1912 5G	0.0973	53.00
1875 to 1933 10G	0.1947	107.00

JAMAICA

Date and Denom.	Fine Gold Content Oz.	Buying Price
1972 $20*	0.2531	140.00
1975, 1976 $100	0.2265	124.00
1978 $100	0.3281	180.00
1978, 1979 $250	1.2507	685.00

PANAMA

Date and Denom.	Fine Gold Content Oz.	Buying Price
1975 to 1979 100B*	0.2361	129.00
1975 to 1979 500B	1.2067	661.00

MEXICO

Date and Denom.	Fine Gold Content Oz.	Buying Price
1945 2p	0.0482	26.00
1945 2 1/2p	0.0602	33.00
1955 5p	0.1205	66.00
1959 10p*	0.2411	132.00
1959 20p	0.4823	265.00
1947 50p	1.2057	660.00

Above dates are restrikes.

RUSSIA

Date and Denom.	Fine Gold Content Oz.	Buying Price
1897 to 1911 5R*	0.1244	68.00
1897 7 1/2R	0.1867	102.00
1898 to 1911 10R	0.2489	136.00
1897 15R	0.3734	205.00
1977 to 1988 100R	0.5000	275.00

IMPORTANT: Buying prices are listed for coins graded VF or better. Bent, damaged or badly worn coins are worth less.

*Coin Illustrated

APPENDIX

BULLION VALUES

Silver and gold coins and other numismatic items are often bought by dealers for their bullion value, that is the value of the pure precious metals which they contain. The weight of precious metals is expressed in grams or troy ounces, not in avoirdupois ounces. A troy ounce is greater than an avoirdupois ounce.

1 Troy Ounce = 31.21035 Grams
1 Avoirdupois Ounce = 28.349 Grams

GOLD

The quantity of pure gold in gold coins is calculated by multiplying the gold fineness or purity of the coin by its weight in troy ounces or grams. Gold purity can also be expressed in karats, a 24-part system with 24-karats equalling pure gold, 22 karats equalling 22 parts gold to 2 parts base metal, 18 karats equalling 18 parts gold to 6 parts base metal etc.

Karats	Fineness	Purity
24	.999	99.9%
22	.916	91.6%
18	.750	75.0%
14	.585	58.5%
10	.417	41.7%
9	.375	37.5%

1 14-karat or .585 fine gold coin weighing 1 troy ounce contains 1 ounce x .585 = .585 troy ounces of pure gold. If gold is worth $600 per troy ounce, then this coin is worth $600 x .585 = $351. (See extended charts on following pages.)

SILVER

The quantity of pure silver in silver coins is calculated by multiplying the silver fineness or purity of the coin by its weight in troy ounces.

Description	Fineness	Purity
Pure	.9999	99.99%
Fine	.999	99.9%
Sterling	.925	92.5%
Coin	.800	80.0%
Coin	.500	50.0%

A .800 fine silver coin weighing 1 troy ounce contains 1 x .800 = .800 troy ounces of pure silver. If silver is worth $20 an ounce, then this coin is worth $20 x .800 = $16. (See extended charts on following pages.)

GOLD CONTENT OF CANADIAN GOLD COIN

Denom.	Date and Mint Mark	Gross Weigh (Grams)	Fineness	Pure Gold Content Grams	Troy Oz.
1 pd.	1908C-1910C	7.99	.917	7.32	.236
1 pd.	1911C-1919C	7.99	.917	7.32	.236
$2	1865-1888	3.33	.917	3.05	.100
$5	1912-1914	8.36	.900	7.52	.242
$10	1912-1914	16.72	.900	15.05	.484
$20	1967	18.27	.900	16.45	.529
$5 M.L.	1982 to date	3.11	.9999	3.11	.100
$10 M.L.	1982 to date	7.78	.9999	7.78	.250
$20 M.L.	1986 to date	15.57	.9999	15.57	.500
$50 M.L.	1979 to date	31.10	.999	31.10	1.000
$100	1976 (Unc.)	13.33	.583	7.78	.250
$100	1976 (Proof)	16.96	.917	15.55	.499
$100	1977-1986	16.96	.917	15.55	.499
$100	1987 to 2003	13.33	.583	7.78	.250
$100	2004 to date	12.00	.583	7.00	.225
$150	2000 to date	11.84	.750	8.88	.285
$175	1992	16.97	.916	15.544	.500
$200	1990 to 2003	17.106	.916	15.669	.500
$200	2004 to date	16.00	.917	14.67	.472
$300	2002 to 2006 (large)	60.00	.583	34.98	1.125
$300	2004 to 2006 (small)	45.00	.583	26.23	.843
$350	1998 to 2003	38.05	.99999	38.05	1.223
$350	2004 to 2006	35.00	.99999	35.00	1.125

SILVER CONTENT OF CANADIAN SILVER COINS

Denom.	Date	Fineness	Silver Content Grams	Troy Oz.
$20	1985-1988	.925	31.103	1.000
$10	1973-1976	.925	44.955	1.445
$5	1973-1976	.925	22.477	.723
$5 M.L.	1987 to date	.999	31.103	1.000
$1	1935-1967	.800	18.661	.600
$1	1971 to date	.500	11.662	.375
50-cents	1870-1919	.925	10.792	.347
50-cents	1920-1967	.800	9.330	.300
25-cents	1870-1919	.925	5.370	.173
25-cents	1920-1967	.800	4.665	.150
25-cents	1967-1968	.500	2.923	.094
10-cents	1858-1919	.925	2.146	.069
10-cents	1920-1967	.800	1.866	.060
10-cents	1967-1968	.500	1.170	.038
5-cents	1858-1919	.925	1.080	.034
5-cents	1920-1921	.800	.933	.030

PLATINUM CONTENT OF CANADIAN PLATINUM COINS

Denom.	Date	Fineness	Platinum Content Grams	Troy Oz.
$300	1990-2004	.9999	31.1	1.000
$150	1990-2004	.9999	15.6	.500
$75	1990-2004	.9999	7.8	.250
$30	1990-2004	.9999	3.1	.100

BULLION VALUES OF CANADIAN GOLD COINS

Computed from $500 to $900 (Canadian dollars) per troy ounce in increments of $100 Canadian.

Denom.	Date and Mint Mark	$500	$600	$700	$800	$900
1 pd.	1908C-1910C	118.00	141.60	165.20	188.80	212.40
1 pd.	1911C-1919C	118.00	141.60	165.20	188.80	212.40
$2	1865-1888	50.00	60.00	70.00	80.00	90.00
$5	1912-1914	121.00	145.20	169.40	193.60	217.80
$10	1912-1914	242.00	290.40	338.80	387.20	435.60
$20	1967	264.50	317.40	370.30	423.20	476.10
$5 M.L.	1982 to date	50.00	60.00	70.00	80.00	90.00
$10 M.L.	1982 to date	125.00	150.00	175.00	200.00	225.00
$20 M.L.	1986 to date	250.00	300.00	350.00	400.00	450.00
$50 M.L.	1979 to date	500.00	600.00	700.00	800.00	900.00
$100	1976 (Unc)	125.00	150.00	175.00	200.00	225.00
$100	1976 (Proof)	250.00	300.00	350.00	400.00	450.00
$100	1977-1986	250.00	300.00	350.00	400.00	450.00
$100	1987 to 2003	125.00	150.00	175.00	200.00	225.00
$100	2004 to date	112.50	135.00	157.50	180.00	202.50
$150	1998 to date	142.50	171.00	200.00	228.00	256.50
$175	1992	250.00	300.00	350.00	400.00	450.00
$200	1990 to 2003	250.00	300.00	350.00	400.00	450.00
$200	2004 to date	236.00	283.20	330.40	377.60	424.80
$300	2002 to 2006 (large)	562.50	675.00	787.50	900.00	1,012.50
$300	2004 to 2006 (small)	421.95	506.35	590.75	675.15	759.50
$350	1998 to 2003	611.50	733.80	856.10	978.40	1,100.70
$350	2004 to 2006	562.65	675.16	787.70	900.20	1,012.75

BULLION VALUES OF CANADIAN SILVER COINS

Computed from $5 to $50 per troy ounce in increments of $10 Canadian.

Denom.	Fineness	$5	$10	$20	$30	$40	$50
$20	.925	5.00	10.00	20.00	30.00	40.00	50.00
$10	.925	7.23	14.00	28.90	43.35	57.80	72.15
$5	.925	3.62	7.23	14.46	21.69	28.92	36.15
$5 M.L.	.999	5.00	10.00	20.00	30.00	40.00	50.00
$1	.800	3.00	6.00	12.00	18.00	24.00	30.00
$1	.500	1.88	3.75	7.50	11.25	15.00	18.75
50 cents	.925	1.74	3.47	6.94	10.41	13.88	17.35
50 cents	.800	1.50	3.00	6.00	9.00	12.00	15.00
25 cents	.925	.87	1.73	3.46	5.19	6.92	8.65
25 cents	.800	.75	1.50	3.00	4.50	6.00	7.50
25 cents	.500	.47	.94	1.88	2.82	3.76	4.70
10 cents	.925	.35	.69	1.38	2.07	2.76	3.45
10 cents	.800	.30	.60	1.20	1.80	2.40	3.00
10 cents	.500	.19	.38	.76	1.14	1.52	1.90
5 cents	.925	.17	.34	.68	1.02	1.36	1.70
5-cents	.800	.15	.30	.60	.90	1.20	1.50

TOREX®
Canada's National Coin Show

Canada's Finest Dealers
In Canadian, Ancient and Foreign Coins, Paper Money, Hobby Supplies, & Reference Books

Show Schedule:
February 24 & 25, 2007
June 23 & 24, 2007
October 27 & 28, 2007

RADISSON ADMIRAL HOTEL
TORONTO – HARBOURFRONT
249 QUEEN'S QUAY WEST
Daily Admission - $6.00

For More Information:
Call: Brian Smith,
(416) 861-9523
Web: www.torex.net
www.canadiancoin.com

WE ARE BUYING!

- Canadian & U.S. Gold and Silver Coins
- Coins, Tokens & Military Medals
- Royal Canadian Mint Products
- Scrap Gold & Silver
- Canadian & U.S. Paper Money

PROOF POSITIVE COINS

P. O. Box 369
BADDECK
Nova Scotia
B0E 1B0

"A positive choice in Canadian Numismatics"

902-295-3007

FREE APPRAISALS!!

We Buy and Sell Across Canada!

We want to purchase your coin and banknote collections!
We are among the top buyers of numismatic material in Canada.
Contact us or Visit our Store.

- Silver coins
- Paper Money
- Gold Coins
- Collector Coins
- USA Coins
- Mint Sets
- Estate Collections
- Silver Bars
- And Much More!

Ask for Todd Sandham

1-888-255-4565

Colonial Acres Coins

300 Victoria St N–Suite #7
Kitchener, ON N2H 6R9
Toll Free 1-888-255-4565
Tel: (519) 579-9048 • Fax: (519) 579-0532
Email: coins@colonialacres.com

$$

TED'S COLLECTABLES INC.

Coins, Paper Money, Pocket Watches,
Jewellery, Postcards Bought & Sold
Estate Appraisals
Investment Coins and Paper Money
available upon request
Buying all Dominion of Canada notes
and
Bank of Canada (1935-1954) notes
Also all CDN, USA and Foreign coins

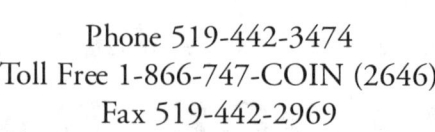

Phone 519-442-3474
Toll Free 1-866-747-COIN (2646)
Fax 519-442-2969
E-mail - tedscollectables@bellnet.ca

$$

NOW OPEN!

AT OUR NEW EXPANDED LOCATION

IMPERIAL COIN AND STAMP CO.

149 KING ST. EAST
HAMILTON, ON
(across from the Ramada Hotel)
905-528-8313

Featuring the Golden Horseshoe's largest display of coins, stamps, sports cards, comic books, Ring Magazines, war medals, Big Little Books, Pulp Magazines and collectibles.

BUYING & SELLING

Come in and see our new arrivals of comic books Vintage and Rare

SEE US IN YOUR TOWN SOON!
DOWNSIZING, SETTLING AN ESTATE, A CHANGE IN LIFESTYLE, MOVING ALL ARE GOOD REASONS TO CALL CANADA'S LARGEST BUYER OF ESTATES

WE CAN OFFER
Immediate hassle-free transactions
Real Buyers with Real Cash Offers
Real Experience with over 25 years of settling estates

1948 Dollar UNC
Paying $800

WE WILL BUY

Coins: Silver, Gold, Copper, Canadian, United States & World
Paper Money: Chartered Notes, Dominion & Bank of Canada
Medals: Military Medals, Badges & Awards
Bullion: Gold, Silver, Platinum, From Scrap to .9999
Diamonds: 1 Carat to 6 Carats, Emerald, Ruby & Sapphire
Jewellery: Antique, Estate & Modern Rings, Bracelets, Necklaces, Earrings, Pendants
Sterling Silver: Tea Sets, Trays, Flatware & Holloware
Doulton, Crown Derby, Worcester, Lladro, Beswick & Swarovski
ROLEX, PATEK PHILIPPE, CARTIER, LECOULTRE, IWC
EATON 1/4 CENTURY, OMEGA, BREITLING, VACHERON
GOLD, STEEL & PLATINUM WATCHES
Wrist Watches: Automatic, Manual Wind, Chiming, Musical Perpetual Calendar, Chronograph, Moonphase, Alarm, etc.
Pocket Watches: Repeater, Chiming, Multi-Coloured Railway 21 Jewels or more, Up & Down, Stop & Complicated

2 Carat D, VS
Paying $20,000

Rolex Daytona
Paying $30,000

We Need U.S. Silver Dollars & Gold Coins!
We Have Investors Waiting.

Some of the Cities We Visit Regularly

Brandon	London	Regina	Toronto
Calgary	Moncton	Saint John	Vancouver
Edmonton	Montreal	Saskatoon	Victoria
Halifax	Ottawa	St. John's	Windsor
Hamilton	Quebec City	Thunder Bay	Winnipeg

For More Information on our Cross-country Buying Events:

Marcus & Company Estate Buyers Inc.
#6 - 1131 Gorham Street, Newmarket, Ontario L3Y 8X9
• By Appointment Only •
Tel: (905)895-5005 • Fax: (905)895-2585
email: info@marcusandcompany.com

We Are Canada's Largest Buyers Because We Pay More